Achieving ISO/IEC
Enabling Change

The 'Achieving ISO/IEC 20000' series

This publication is the sixth in a series of ten publications related to ISO/IEC 20000. Each publication provides advice on different aspects of ISO/IEC 20000. The books in the 'Achieving ISO/IEC 20000' series are:

> *Management decisions and documentation* (BIP 0030)
>
> *Why people matter* (BIP 0031)
>
> *Making metrics work* (BIP 0032)
>
> *Managing end-to-end service* (BIP 0033)
>
> *Finance for service managers* (BIP 0034)
>
> *Enabling change* (BIP 0035)
>
> *Keeping the service going* (BIP 0036)
>
> *Capacity management* (BIP 0037)
>
> *Integrated service management* (BIP 0038)
>
> *The differences between BS 15000 and ISO/IEC 20000* (BIP 0039)

This series provides practical guidance and advice on introducing IT service management best practice in accordance with ISO/IEC 20000. More details on the content of each publication are given in *Books in the 'Achieving ISO/IEC 20000' series*, at the end of this book.

Although security issues are covered in ISO/IEC 20000, the 'Achieving ISO/IEC 20000' series does not cover security requirements. Information on security can be found in the BSI publications that are listed in the *Bibliography* in Appendix B.

Other publications

BSI also publishes:

A managers' guide to service management (BIP 0005) is intended for managers who are new to support services or who are faced with major changes to their existing support facility. This book takes the form of informative explanations, guidance and recommendations.

IT service management – Self-assessment workbook (BIP 0015) is an easy to use checklist that complements ISO/IEC 20000 and is designed to assist an organization's internal assessment of their services and the extent to which they conform to the specified requirements in ISO/IEC 20000.

Achieving ISO/IEC 20000
Enabling Change

Dr Jenny Dugmore and Shirley Lacy

BSi
Business
Information

First published in the UK in 2006

by
BSI
389 Chiswick High Road
London W4 4AL

Typeset in Frutiger by Typobatics Limited
Printed in Great Britain by Formara Limited

British Library Cataloguing in Publication Data
A catalogue record for this book is available from the British Library

ISBN 0-580-44639-5

Contents

Foreword

Organizations are under increasing pressure to gain a competitive advantage, manage operational risks and increase profitability and/or maintain growth. Achieving these business goals requires constant business and technology change. However, making changes is often difficult due to the distributed nature and complexity of the end-to-end services. If changes are not well understood and managed they result in unacceptable operational risks and service degradation.

Change, configuration and release management enable organizations to make changes that meet the business and customer needs at the agreed cost, at the right time and in a controlled manner. To achieve this organizations need a good understanding of their IT services and the underlying infrastructure.

This book explains the requirements for the configuration, change and release management processes which are contained in three ISO/IEC 20000-1 clauses. These processes are important for service providers in controlling the production environment and aligning their services with the business needs. The book explains the role of these processes and how the processes interface with each other. It includes example metrics and audit evidence with practical hints, tips and techniques that will help a service provider achieve the requirements.

The book also explains the relationship between the three processes, the Plan-Do-Check-Act cycle and the planning and implementing of new or changed services.

Dr Jenny Dugmore

Acknowledgements

This book has been produced with the input and assistance of people involved in the practical aspects of delivering services across all sectors and those involved in the production of both BS 15000 and ISO/IEC 20000. We would like to thank them for sharing their views and providing constructive criticism, case studies and practical techniques.

It is not possible to list all of those who have helped, but particular thanks goes to:

Alison Holt of Synergy International; Barbara Eastman; Bedelia Wolverton; Dave Church; David Cuthbertson of Square Mile Systems; Debbi Church; Gene Webb; Gerald Mulhern of Apertil Consultancy; Louise Howson of Xansa; Lynda Cooper of Fox IT; Maxine Carter of the Financial Times; Paul Green of Capita; Perveen Jassal of the Financial Times; Robert Cowham of Vaccaperna; Robert Thomas; Seema Arora of the Financial Times; Sunil P. Rangreji of Wipro Technologies; and Sylvia Prickel of Agilita;

Finally, we would like to thank Simone Levy and Kieran Parkinson of BSI for their support, helpful suggestions, tact and patience with the production of the 'Achieving ISO/IEC 20000' series.

INTRODUCTION

What is ISO/IEC 20000?

ISO/IEC 20000 is the first IT service management process standard to be produced by the International Organization for Standardization (ISO), and it is based on the knowledge and experience gained by experts working in the field.

ISO/IEC 20000 was produced by Technical Committee ISO/IEC JTC 1/SC 7, *Software and system engineering*, and was based on BS 15000, which was produced by BSI Technical Committee BDD/3, *Information services management*.

ISO/IEC 20000 is in two parts.

* ISO/IEC 20000-1 is a specification containing requirements that must be met in order to achieve ISO/IEC 20000.
* ISO/IEC 20000-2 is a code of practice on how to achieve the requirements in ISO/IEC 20000-1.

The requirements in Part 1 (i.e. ISO/IEC 20000-1) are applicable to service providers of all sizes and types, regardless of whether the organization is public or private sector, internal or external. The recommendations in Part 2 (i.e. ISO/IEC 20000-2) are optional approaches to achieving the requirements in Part 1. Although optional, the recommendations are also practical and proven methods that are normally appropriate.

The purpose of ISO/IEC 20000

ISO/IEC 20000 provides the basis for assessing whether service providers have best practice, reliable, repeatable and measurable processes applied consistently across their organization. As a process-based standard the requirements are independent of organizational structure or of the tools used to automate the service management processes. ISO/IEC 20000-1 provides the basis for formal certification schemes and other audits.

The 'Achieving ISO/IEC 20000' series

The 'Achieving ISO/IEC 20000' series is designed to explain the requirements of ISO/IEC 20000. An abstract of the ISO/IEC 20000 clauses that are most relevant to the topic of 'Enabling change' is given in Appendix A. Also, Table 1 provides a clause-by-clause guide to the content of each of the books in the 'Achieving ISO/IEC 20000' series.

This sixth publication in the 'Achieving ISO/IEC 20000' series covers the processes that enable the service provider to successfully change the services and IT infrastructure across the supply chain. This book describes how the processes interface with each other. It includes example metrics and audit evidence with practical tips, techniques and case studies that will help a service provider understand and achieve the requirements of ISO/IEC 20000 for the configuration, change and release management processes.

Additional advice

Service providers aiming for ISO/IEC 20000 may find it useful to seek advice on best practice, the qualifications that are available for individual service management professionals and ISO/IEC 20000 certification. Details of these can be found via the web pages in Appendix B.

Table 1 – Clause-by-clause guide to the 'Achieving ISO/IEC 20000' series

ISO/IEC 20000 clause	BIP 0030	BIP 0031	BIP 0032	BIP 0033	BIP 0034	BIP 0035	BIP 0036	BIP 0037	BIP 0038	BIP 0039
Terms and definitions	▓									▓
Management responsibility	▓	▓							▓	▓
Documentation requirements	▓	▓								▓
Competence, awareness and training		▓							▓	▓
Planning and implementing service management	▓								▓	▓
Plan – Do – Check – Act cycle	▓									▓
Planning and implementing new or changed services										▓
Service level management				▓						▓
Service reporting			▓							▓
Service continuity and availability management							▓			▓
Budgeting and accounting for IT services					▓					▓
Information security management					See BSI publications on information security management in the BIP 0070 series					▓
Capacity management								▓		▓
Business relationship management				▓						▓
Supplier management				▓						▓
Incident management							▓			▓
Problem management							▓			▓
Configuration management						▓				▓
Change management						▓				▓
Release management										▓

CHAPTER 1

Enabling change

Introduction

Organizations are constantly changing. There are many different types of change, such as business improvements, legal and regulatory changes, mergers, acquisitions and daily operational changes to keep services running.

A service provider[1] that is capable of making changes quickly and reliably provides significant business advantages.

ISO/IEC 20000-1 requires a service provider to align services with business needs. A service provider also needs to understand the existing services and the environment within which existing services operate in order to understand the risk and impact of changes.

Meeting the ISO/IEC 20000 requirements for the configuration, change and release management processes enables a service provider to:

- contribute to meeting corporate governance, legal, contractual and regulatory requirements;
- effectively prioritize and respond to proposals for change;
- maintain, control and understand the state of its services and infrastructure;
- reduce failed changes and releases;
- contribute to estimating and controlling the cost of change;
- establish a low risk introduction approach for new services;
- keep software current e.g. security patches;
- achieve significant cost benefits from reduction in duplication of resources and under utilization of existing assets;
- achieve a reduction in investment for redundant /or unnecessary assets;
- eliminate the use of illegal software within the organization.

---

[1] The service provider is the organization aiming to achieve ISO/IEC 20000.

An overview of the requirements for the following three processes is given in this chapter and in more detail in Chapters 2 to 4:

- configuration management (Part 1, clause 9.1);
- change management (Part 1, clause 9.2);
- release management (Part 1, clause 10.1).

An ISO/IEC 20000 auditor's main interest in the processes is to check that best practices have been implemented and that each requirement in ISO/IEC 20000 is met. ISO/IEC 20000-1 does not require a service provider to use the terms used in ISO/IEC 20000, although there must be no ambiguity about what each process includes. It is usually easier for a service provider to adopt common industry terms. If this has not been done, an ISO/IEC 20000 auditor will find it useful to have a mapping of the service provider's terms with those used in ISO/IEC 20000. This will simplify the audit.

Configuration management

The objective of the configuration management process is to define and control the components of the service and infrastructure. By maintaining accurate configuration information the configuration management process ensures that the current state of the services and infrastructure is known, including a history of the services and infrastructure. It also means that only authorized components are used and only authorized changes are made. This process is covered in greater detail in Chapter 3.

Change management

The objective of the change management process is to ensure all changes are assessed, approved, implemented and reviewed in a controlled manner. This enables the service provider to minimize the risk of disruption to the services. The change management process handles proposed and actual changes to components. It also ensures that the service provider works with the business, customers, suppliers and stakeholders to prioritize and deliver changes that have maximum benefit first. This helps the service provider to align the services with the business needs. This process is covered in greater detail in Chapter 4.

Release management

The release management process ensures that a release moves efficiently through the development life cycle and is then successfully rolled out to all target environments, machines, locations and users. The process includes planning, design and logistics. The process includes the mechanisms to handle, package, distribute, install and deliver all the components of the release efficiently. Effective release management can significantly improve a service provider's ability to handle high volumes of change. This process is described in Chapter 5.

Definitions

Release

A release is a special case of a CI, composed of a set of CIs being changed.

Asset[2]

Assets have a cash value, typically 'things that have been bought or built'. Assets may be CIs, form part of a CI or may be composed of several CIs. Not all CIs are assets.

Change record

A change record is a record containing details of which CIs are affected and how they are affected by an authorized change.

Configuration

A configuration is an arrangement of parts or elements and their relative position within a system, e.g. the relative positions of the stars and planets in the solar system, or all the components in an airplane.

Configuration Item (CI)

A component that is identified, tracked and controlled by the configuration management process. CIs may vary widely in complexity, size, status and type, ranging from an entire system including all hardware, software module and documentation, to a single module or a minor hardware component. A CI may contain other CIs.

Configuration management database (CMDB)

A CMDB is a database containing all the relevant details of each CIs and details of the important relationships between them. The CMDB may be a single physical repository or several repositories linked so that they can be used as if they were a single database, i.e. a single logical repository.

Request for change (or change request)

A form or screen used to record details of a request for a change to any CI within a service or infrastructure.

Roll out

The term 'roll out' is used for the deployment of a release to customers, users or target environments.

---

[2] Definition of 'Asset' is a summary of that given in BIP 0034, *Finance for service managers.*

How the three processes work together

Service management is only effective if the processes are integrated, as described in BIP 0038, *Integrated service management*. If the processes in this book are not integrated then the service provider will struggle to maintain accurate configuration information in the CMDB as the services and infrastructure change. This results in bad information so that mistakes are made that require re-work.

The configuration management process provides reliable information used in the planning and implementation of changes and releases. The configuration management process in turn relies on the change management and release processes to provide updates to the configuration information.

The release management process is typically used to implement one or more related changes that can be tested and rolled out together.

Figure 1 provides an example of the main information flows between the processes in this book. For the sake of simplicity interfaces to other processes are not shown. Figure 1 shows:

- change requests to be incorporated into a release are identified by the configuration management process;
- information from the configuration management process is used by the change management process for defining, planning, assessing, scheduling, coordinating, reviewing and by checking changes.

The configuration management information in the CMDB is updated by the change management process as the CIs change status, characteristics or ownership. An audit trail of all changes to CIs is included in the CMDB. The request for change is related to the new version of a release and related CIs.

The release management process uses configuration information when planning a release. As a release goes through the stages of acceptance testing and then roll out to users the configuration information is updated.

The definitive versions of the software and documentation release are copied from a secure library back into the development environment, where it is used to make changes. As new versions of software and documentation pass the relevant quality checks and are rolled out, new definitive versions are copied into the secure libraries.

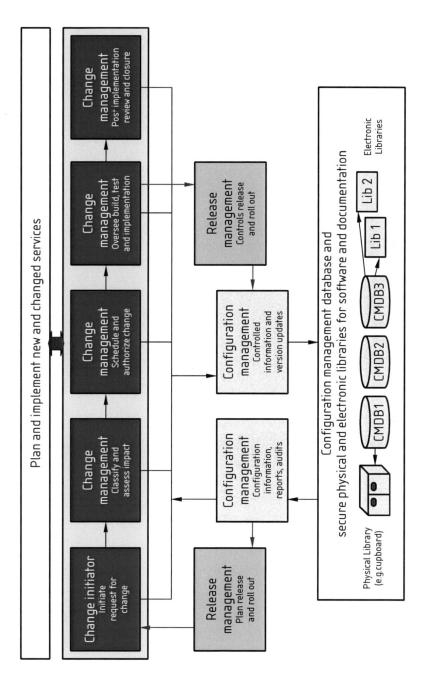

Figure 1 - Example of process integration

CHAPTER 2

Configuration management (ISO/IEC 20000-1, 9.1)

Introduction

This chapter describes the key features of the configuration management process required to meet the objective:

'To define and control the components of the service and infrastructure and maintain accurate configuration information'.

The ISO/IEC 20000 requirements for the configuration management process can be summarized as:

- selecting and defining configuration items (CIs);
- ensuring that only authorized CIs are used;
- maintaining the integrity of systems and services;
- accurate configuration management information in the CMDB;
- providing access to configuration information, with different views;
- verifying and auditing CIs for nonconformances.

What is effective configuration management?

The process is only effective if there is clear accountability and ownership for all CIs with clearly defined responsibilities, for example clarity on roles such as changing CIs and updating the CMDB and related information.

An effective configuration management process provides the configuration information and procedures to plan, maintain and track all changes to CIs. The process therefore provides a suitable audit trail of all changes.

An effective configuration management process provides different views of the current and planned state of the services and infrastructure for different roles.

This helps those involved to:

- relate technical components to services and to business needs;
- understand the risk and impact of changes;
- identify the root cause of incidents and problems;
- find configuration information quickly.

An effective process also allows the service provider to trace changes back to the original request for change. This is particularly useful when a change fails or a problem is being investigated.

It also helps the identification of nonconformances in the infrastructure and services, such as:

- CIs that do not meet requirements;
- components that may need to be replaced;
- CIs changed without authorization.

The scope and level of detail for configuration information are both important for an effective configuration management process.

If the scope is too wide because far too much detail is held about CIs, effort will be wasted in maintaining information that is of no practical use. If there is too little detail there will be a lack of control and lack of visibility required for effective use of the information by other service management processes.

ISO/IEC 20000-2 recommends that an appropriate level of automation is implemented to ensure that processes are not inefficient, error prone or ignored. In practice the configuration management process requires some level of automation for all but small scale services and infrastructures.

Scope of configuration management and CIs

Although the scope of the CIs used for the service and infrastructure for different service providers may be very different, the minimum scope is:

- services defined in the service catalogue[3];
- CIs required to deliver the services e.g. desktops;
- software and licenses;
- CIs in the underlying infrastructure that require maintenance;

---

[3] This term is often used for a repository of information on the services, in business terms, established by the service level management and business relationship management processes.

Reducing the scope of the CIs under the control of the configuration management process to less than this would mean the service provider cannot meet the requirements of ISO/IEC 20000.

Context and requirements

The context and requirements for the configuration management process must be based on the service provider's and customer's business drivers. The process must also support policies and standards and meet the requirements of the other service management processes. This provides evidence that the configuration management process has been planned to minimize the risk of failure and to reflect service criticality.

Table 2 – Mapping back to the business requirement

Business requirement	Configuration management requirement
Legal regulations for the use of software assets	All software assets and related assets are identified and managed in countries where the legal regulations apply
Sarbanes-Oxley Act – control of core business processes that are fundamental to the financials of the company	All IT assets required for financial management are identified and managed. Components that support the security and integrity of data for financial processes will be uniquely identified and will be traceable back to their original requirement
Reduce the operational risks to critical services	CIs will be classified by high, medium, low risk. High risk items will include: • new technology within the organization; • items that cause major incidents; • items that cause outages; • single points of failure; • external interfaces; • internal interfaces; • security perimeter

External interface controls

ISO/IEC 20000-2 recommends that the service provider should integrate the configuration, change and release processes with the other processes and those of its customers and suppliers.

To achieve this it is recommended that a service provider formally agrees requirements for the configuration, change and release management processes. This is with the customer via the business relationship management processes and with suppliers via the supplier management process. The service level management process would normally be involved as this is a key process linking suppliers, the service provider and customers.

In the case of suppliers, it is the service provider's responsibility to define any requirements placed on suppliers. The service provider must retain overall control of suppliers and any of the supplier's processes that cross the supplier-service provider organizational interface. This applies even if the service provider's processes and procedures are tailored to accommodate a supplier's environment. These requirements are passed formally to the supplier via the supplier management process.

ISO/IEC 20000-2 recommends that the configuration management plan includes the approach to managing suppliers and subcontractors performing configuration management. Configuration management planning usually includes the validation of a supplier's process, procedures and documentation. Typically this is achieved through reports from the supplier on their performance, and periodic inspections of suppliers' actual activities. The aim is to ensure that the supplier continues to follow the agreed processes and procedures. The interfaces between a service provider and its customers and suppliers are illustrated in Figure 2

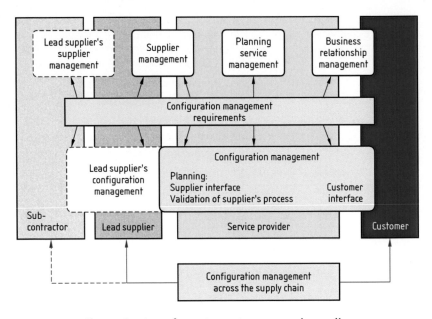

Figure 2 – Interfaces to customers and suppliers

Example: Asset vs. configuration management

An organization with an in-house service provider had a database with financial and asset information on PCs and PC software. This was used by both the finance department and the service provider and was managed and maintained to a high standard.

To meet the best practice requirements of ISO/IEC 20000-1, the service provider needed to add information on its services and the central infrastructure. This was necessary to provide an end-to-end view of the configuration items (CIs) used to deliver each service. After investigating various options the service provider decided to keep the asset database and add a commercially available package that included a CMDB.

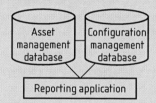

Figure 3 – An example process map for a reporting tool documenting database discrepancies

Duplication of actual data was minimized. Where duplication of CI data was required the change, configuration and release management procedures made it clear where the definitive version of the CI data was held and where updates needed to be performed. The databases were synchronized regularly. An automated check on CIs was performed each night by the configuration management process. This checked the discrepancies between the data recorded in the CMDB and the actual CIs that were detected by the overnight check. A reporting tool documented the discrepancies and also gave information on what assets and CIs were held by the two databases (see Figure 3).

Key point:

An auditor will not be concerned if a database that is used as an asset database for financial (or legal) purposes is also used by the configuration management process, as long as the database and how it is used by the configuration management process meets the requirements of ISO/IEC 20000.

The organization recognized the need to manage duplication of configuration information and make information easily accessible to staff with the customized reports, meeting the requirements of ISO/IEC 20000.

Mapping to financial asset accounting

ISO/IEC 20000-1 includes a note[4] that the financial asset accounting process falls outside the scope of the configuration management process. However there is also a note in ISO/IEC 20000-1 that recommends that the service provider should define the interface between configuration management and the financial asset accounting processes.

It is often useful to map the types of CI used by the configuration management process to the asset types used in financial management as this helps to align and integrate the two processes. Not all CIs are assets but all assets will be CIs or composed of CIs.

ISO/IEC 20000-1 requirements include the management of assets required to deliver the services, as well as the management of other CIs. For example, information on how the CIs used for a desktop service are connected helps to determine the business impact of a proposed change to a desktop application.

Configuration management planning

ISO/IEC 20000-1, 9.1 requires an integrated approach to planning of the change and configuration management processes.

An auditor may review the configuration management plan as the first step in auditing the change and configuration management processes, and how the plan is implemented in practice. This may involve checks to ensure that an integrated approach was adopted for planning both the change and configuration management processes

ISO/IEC 20000-2 recommends that there is an up-to-date configuration management plan to cover the management of all CIs. The configuration management plan is part of the service provider's overall service management plan for the service provider. More details on this are provided in BIP 0038, *Integrated service management*.

Contents of a configuration management plan

The configuration management plan may cross-refer to other documents that provide details e.g. requirements for configuration management, process and procedure documents. An example contents list for a configuration management plan is given below.

---

[4] A NOTE in Part 1 is not part of the requirements. A NOTE offers an explanation of the requirements or is a recommendation and is therefore similar in meaning to text in the Code of Practice (Part 2).

Example: Configuration management plan contents list

Objectives

Scope

For example, applicable services, infrastructure, and/or locations.

Applicable policies and standards, including ISO/IEC 20000

Requirements

- Link to business and service management requirements.

- Requirements for accountability, traceability, and auditability.

Configuration management activities

- Configuration identification.

- Configuration control.

- Configuration status accounting.

- Configuration verification and audit.

Roles and responsibilities

Interface controls

- With financial asset management.

- With suppliers, projects, development and testing.

- With customers.

Management of suppliers and sub-contractors

Resources

- For bringing assets and configurations under control.

- For maintaining the configuration management system/CMDB.

Link to training plan

Automation

- Version control.

- Discovery, detection and auditing tools.

- Build and installation tools.

Configuration management roles

Typical roles involved in configuration management are:

- Configuration management process owner (described in Chapter 6);

- CI owner/custodian e.g. for a service or for local assets;

- Configuration management architect /designer;

- Configuration analyst;

- Configuration administrator/configuration librarian.

Generic roles are also used as well e.g. developer, implementer. Each role is linked to a set of activities and usually to a stage in the lifecycle of CIs.

What is configuration identification?

ISO/IEC 20000-1 requires the service provider to have a policy on what is defined as a CI and also on each CI's constituent components. This is usually achieved by defining the constituent components for each type of CI as described in this section.

The **configuration identification** process ensures that all affected organizations have common sets of configuration **information** as the basis for managing and supporting the services and infrastructure.

Data on individual CIs are the building blocks of information essential to service management. If the selection of CIs and how they are related and grouped is too complex, too simple or illogical, the information will be difficult to use and its use will not be effective. Many issues are caused by poor selection, grouping and definition of CIs. A configuration management process based on a badly designed set of CIs is unlikely to meet the requirements of ISO/IEC 20000-1.

Classifying CIs

CIs are usually classified by type and each type is linked to a standard life cycle such as the examples shown in Table 3.

Table 3 – Examples of CI lifecycles by CI type

CI types	Example life cycles for CI types				
Service	Acceptance test	Pilot	In-service	Retired	
Hardware	Ordered	Commissioned	Live	In store	Retired
Application release	Acquired	Acceptance test	Live	Retired	
Service document	Draft	Approved	Issued	Superseded	

Selecting and grouping CIs

The configuration management process includes identification, tracking and control of CIs.

This involves selection, definition and grouping of CIs to get the best balance between the information needs of service management as a whole and the cost of keeping the information accurate and current. Conversely, the correct approach to identifying CIs provides the foundation for effective configuration control, status accounting, verification and audit.

An ISO/IEC 20000 auditor may check that the CIs are chosen using established selection criteria that are grouped, classified and identified in such a way that they are manageable and traceable throughout their lifecycle.

Many configuration management process owners define the services and infrastructure as logically-related and subordinate groups of CIs. This helps to define the ownership hierarchy of CIs. An example is shown in Figure 4 using the example of an email service. Examples of the documentation for a service are shown in the section on *Defining configuration documentation*.

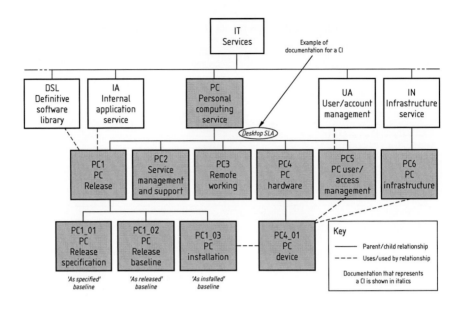

Figure 4 – An example of the constituent parts of a personal computing service

Relationships

CIs that are used by service management processes but which are outside the control of the service provider are usually identified by information such as 'X is used by Y'. It is advisable for information held on this type of CI to make it easy to identify who does control these CIs.

There is an ISO/IEC 20000-1 requirement that the configuration management process also defines the documentation for CIs. This provides information for other service management processes. This information is important for impact analysis and root cause analysis of problems by the problem management process.

Typical relationships used in the identification of CIs are:

- parent;
- child/comprises;
- used/used by;
- made of;
- connected to;
- impacts/impacted by;

- change request – affected CI/version;

- change request – implemented CI/version;

- known error – CI/version that caused a problem.

Some of these relationships are shown in Figure 4. For example, PC is the parent CI of PC1 to PC6 and PC1_01 is the parent of 4 CIs, shown as the next level in the hierarchy. PC1_01 uses the definitive software library (DSL) and internal application service (IA).

CI information

ISO/IEC 20000-1 requires the service provider to define what information is to be recorded for each type of CI. This typically includes the following:

- unique identifier;

- CI type;

- name/description;

- version (e.g. file, build, baseline, release);

- location;

- owner/custodian;

- status;

- supplier/source;

- related document masters;

- related software masters;

- related CIs;

- related changes;

- related problems and known errors;

- audit trail.

ISO/IEC 20000-1 also requires that the attributes that describe the specific functional and physical characteristics of each type of CI are defined e.g. size, capacity.

Defining configuration documentation

The characteristics of a CI are often documented. For example, the service requirements specification and service level agreement for a service describe the characteristics of a CI which is a service.

Many organizations specify mandatory and optional documents that describe a CI.

Table 4 – Types of CI and related documentation

CI type	Related information for a CI
Customer service	• Service requirements specification • Service level requirement specification • Service level agreement • Service report template
External suppliers service	• Contract • Service level agreement (contract schedule) • Supplier's service management plan • Process interface definition • Contact list • Shared data environment
Application	• Application release policy • Application requirements specification • Application design specification • Application release acceptance test plan • Application technical environment specification • Application release acceptance test report • Application release documentation • Application release software • Application 'release to production' baseline • Application license master documentation
Application installation	• Application license • Application installation record

Example: The level of detail for configuration information

A service provider was starting to implement configuration management and staff were too optimistic about the level of configuration information that could be maintained. They planned to convert network diagrams into the CMDB, but encountered difficulties very quickly.

The recently appointed configuration management process owner held a requirements workshop. It was agreed that the network diagram would instead be held in a master document library and accessed via a hyperlink.

The following criteria were defined to help agree the optimum level of detail in the future.

- Who wants what information and when?

- What format is required for storage and presentation e.g. text, diagram or photograph?

- What information is mandatory for effective control?

- Who will do updates through the CI life cycle?

- Is the information relevant and auditable?

- Where appropriate is data held in a textual format, e.g. XML rather than binary to enable comparison and verification?

- How CIs will be marked and recorded in the CMDB?

- What relationships and dependencies are required to provide the necessary control?

Key point:

The level of configuration information to be held is important for an effective and efficient process. The configuration management process owner needs to be a good facilitator, have a practical approach and be firm about the approach to managing configuration information.

Example: Ineffective vs. effective configuration management

A service provider tracked the base unit, monitor, keyboard and mouse for 10,000 personal computers and over 100 central servers. As there were insufficient staff to maintain the information with the current level of service management automation two key improvements were identified.

The service provider decided that it was only realistic for them to track the base units. However, there were a few expensive monitors that had to be tracked for financial asset management and a few specialist keyboards that were difficult and expensive to replace. As a result these were included in the tracking and the information was maintained by the configuration management process. The service provider reduced the number of CIs from 40,000 to 10,500.

The service provider was maintaining information on central servers and their external supplier of hardware maintenance services also maintained server information on their own CMDB.

It was agreed that the supplier would maintain the master record of the server hardware that they maintained and an automatic feed would be implemented to update the service provider's CMDB.

Key point:

Agreeing the scope of configuration management and defining the CIs to the right level was recognized as important. It was realized that the alternative was time wasted trying to update information that is either not required or which can be provided by a supplier.

Auditable markings

ISO/IEC 20000-2 recommends that configuration information should include auditable markings or other methods of identification for CIs. This identifier is then recorded in the CMDB. For each type of CI an auditor may seek evidence of:

- the naming conventions;
- data definitions;
- how the physical or electronic component is labelled;
- where the CI is physically located.

It is important to identify the information to be recorded at each state in a CI's life cycle. Often configuration information is updated when a CI is moved to the next state. The correct level of configuration information detail is important for the configuration management process to be effective. If the information is too detailed then resources will be wasted in maintaining information that is unnecessary. If the level of detail is not sufficient there will be a lack of control and a lack of the visibility required for effective service management.

Configuration baselines

ISO/IEC 20000-1 requires a snapshot of CIs, usually referred to as a baseline, to be taken before a release of new or changed CIs into the live environment. The baseline is used for audits of CIs as described in the section on *Verification and audit*. The baseline information must therefore be suitable for this purpose. For example, where software installations are automated it is best practice to baseline the software that is already installed before the new software is released. This provides a good basis for comparison of the configuration before and after the release.

This configuration baseline also enables a change or release to be reversed correctly or a service to be recovered in the event of a disaster.

The role of the CMDB

ISO/IEC 20000-1 includes a requirement that every CI managed by the configuration management process can be identified and that the details on it are recorded in a database, which ISO/IEC 20000 refers to as the configuration management data base (CMDB).

Financial processes (covered in BIP 0034, *Finance for service managers*) may only need to know how many of each type of item there are for accounting purposes. Service management also needs to know where they are, how they fit in with everything else, what changes have been made to them and what changes are planned.

In smaller service providers a set of spreadsheets may be all that is required for a 'fit for purpose' CMDB. However, even if spreadsheets are adequate for an individual service provider it is not acceptable for there to be duplicated or conflicting data in different spreadsheets.

An ISO/IEC 20000 auditor would normally interpret duplicated data that was conflicting or was the result of unmanaged duplication as evidence that the configuration management process is ineffective. An auditor may also interpret this as evidence that the Plan-Do-Check-Act (PDCA) cycle was deficient in some way.

At the organization level, the data for CIs used across the organization will often be maintained in a primary database. This may be labelled as the 'Service Management Primary Database', as in Figures 5 and 6. This may be supplemented by linked databases that hold the details for specific types of CIs e.g. software, desktop and/or network. Typical options for the relationships between multiple databases are shown in Figures 5 and 6. In both cases a portal is provided for staff to easily find the configuration information and carry out updates.

In the example in Figure 5 there are inputs from 'Corporate Systems', such as employee information, and from the 'Programme and Project Management System', such as target release dates. The 'Corporate Systems' updates the 'User Database' that is linked to and also accessible from the 'Service Management Primary Database'. This primary database has the master records for high level configuration items. Further detail is accessible in the lower level databases. In the example in Figure 5 the software and document management system is also shared with the 'Engineering' department.

In Figure 6 automatic updates are received from the 'Human Resources', 'Finance and Procurement' and 'Development Configuration Management' systems. The primary database again has the master records for high level configuration items and further detail is again accessible in the lower level databases. Records for master copies of the service and quality documentation are in the 'Service Management Primary Database'. These have hyperlinks to the document management system.

Physical and electronic libraries

ISO/IEC 20000-1 requires that master copies of CIs, such as software and documentation, which are usually referred to as digital CIs, are controlled in secure physical or electronic libraries. References to the libraries are included in the CMDB.

Electronic libraries generally include both software libraries and document libraries. Physical libraries include hard copy storage areas such as fire-proof safes, cupboards or filing cabinets.

Although physically separate from the rest of the CMDB these electronic and physical libraries form part of a logical repository of configuration information. It is important that staff can quickly locate the definitive versions of software and documentation for use in service management.

Figure 7 shows two physical databases that are labelled 'Shared CMDB01' and 'Software CMDB02'. Figure 7 also shows the links between these two physical databases and the secure electronic and physical libraries that contain definitive versions of software and documentation.

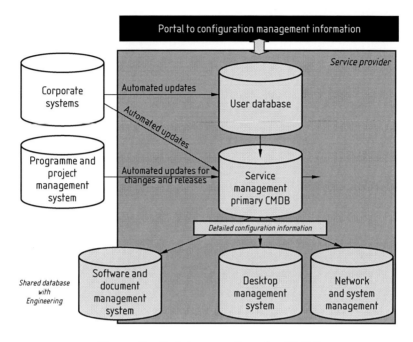

Figure 5 – Database options for CMDB

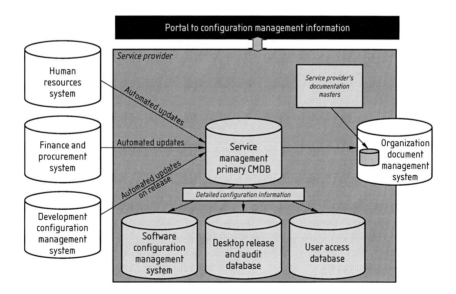

Figure 6 – Database options for CMDB

The CMDB records references to the definitive version of the document or software object in the relevant library. In Figure 7 the 'Document Library 07' is a cupboard that contains hard copy versions of master documents such as signed contracts and software licenses.

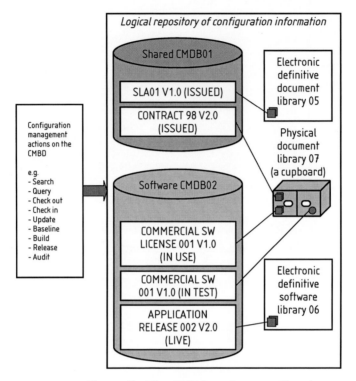

Figure 7 – The CMDB and secure libraries

An ISO/IEC 20000 auditor may ask to see a list of all the physical databases and secure libraries that are linked to the CMDB and how they are logically linked.

Access controls

Many of the service provider's staff require access to the CMDB for their role in service management. This information must be protected during access, for example from unauthorized creation of CIs or unauthorized changes to CIs. Other controls may be required, such as preventing access to personal information used to update the CMDB in Figure 7. Access controls vary depending on the type of activity e.g. creating, changing or removing a CI. For example, staff can be given the correct level of access to the CMDB by control of the hardware, software, media and documentation.

An ISO/IEC 20000 auditor will not seek evidence of a specific method of access control but will expect to see that the controls are appropriate and that there are no loopholes, such as staff that have changed roles retaining their original access rights.

It is best practice to standardize and define the roles that are responsible for updating information at each stage of a CI's lifecycle and for change records. Many configuration management tools use this mechanism to ensure that only appropriate staff can update the information at certain points in the process.

Checking information to identify and then correct errors in the CMDB is described in more detail in the sections on *Configuration control* and *Status accounting.*

Controlled hardware

Although not specifically required by ISO/IEC 20000, it is usually advisable for hardware CIs to be held in controlled storage areas. Sometimes these are called the definitive hardware store.

They are typically used for:

- hardware to be protected from damage or tampering;
- PCs required for controlled builds;
- important spares that may be needed at short notice e.g. for a business critical server.

Configuration control

It is a requirement of ISO/IEC 20000 that the integrity of systems, services and service components is maintained by procedures controlling CIs. Configuration control enables this by ensuring an authorized person updates the information in the CMDB as changes are made to CIs e.g. changes in the status, location, ownership and version.

Staff need to be clear on exactly what control procedure to apply in particular circumstances. For example there may be different installation procedures for different computing platforms and staff need to select the right procedure to follow.

ISO/IEC 20000-2 recommends that only authorized CIs are accepted and recorded from receipt to disposal. This is illustrated in the example 'Implementing configuration control procedures'.

Example: Implementing configuration control procedures

A government organization wanted to ensure that the ISO/IEC 20000 configuration control requirements and recommendations would be met. They had overlapping procedures for installing upgrades, patches and other changes. It was difficult to see if the CMDB was being updated at the appropriate points.

The following checklist was used on internal audits to check how CIs are controlled and how the related information is updated when:

- a new CI is acquired/registered;

- a new version of a CI is acquired/registered;

- the state of a CI changes;

- a CI is changed;

- a version of a CI is updated;

- a CI is released;

- a CI is withdrawn or disposed/retired;

- a CI is built into another CI;

- controlled electronic objects or files are copied or moved.

A matrix was used to define which types of CI used which control procedures and when. Gaps were identified and the procedures were restructured.

Key point:

With poorly structured procedures it can be difficult for a service provider to prove that the configuration data is updated at the right time. The service provider will need to provide evidence that CI information is updated as changes are made.

Automation

Version management or library management software is commonly used to produce audit trails of document and software changes and to maintain version numbers, creation date information and copies of previous versions.

Many service providers use a configuration management system that provides functions to:

- manually update data, typically with validation of input data;

- automatically update data e.g. baseline the CIs in a release;

- automatically update data from external tools.

Other tools that are commonly used to automate the configuration management are:

- build tools;

- baseline and comparison tools;

- installation and de-installation tools;

- discovery and audit tools;

- detection of nonconformances and recovery tools.

It is usually advisable that these tools and configuration control procedures automate updates to CI records/CMDB wherever possible. This generally increases the accuracy. For example, when a desktop release is made to 25,000 users, if a desktop distribution tool is used it should automatically update the CMDB when installation on each user's desktop has been completed satisfactorily.

Status accounting

Status accounting of CIs provides the audit trail of changes to a CI as it progresses through its life cycle e.g. ordered, in stock, live, disposed. It also ensures that the status of CIs is visible to all those that need the information and is required by ISO/IEC 20000-1.

The information for status accounting includes information about any uniquely identifiable CI throughout the life cycle of that CI. It includes the capture, storage, retrieval and access of information necessary to account for the configuration of a service, the infrastructure or constituent configuration items. The information is captured in the CMDB. An audit trail is established when a CI is first changed and the audit trail is then updated after each subsequent change.

All configuration management activities provide information to the status accounting activity. It also includes baselines such as:

- 'as-specified' configuration;

- 'as-designed' configuration;

- 'as-released' configuration;

- 'as-installed' configuration.

ISO/IEC 20000-2 recommends that the service provider should be able to collate the status of CIs that together constitute:

- a service, configuration or system;
- a change, baseline, build or release;
- version or variant of a configuration item.

To achieve this it is sometimes necessary to baseline the CIs and place the baseline report under the control of the configuration management process.

Status accounting information demonstrates that the service provider is in control of its CIs by providing evidence such as:

- CIs are traceable;
- CIs are auditable by the configuration management process;
- information on CIs is available to the change management process;
- a baseline of CI data was captured before a release.

An example of a configuration status report is shown in Table 5. In this example of a status report the CI type of APP_REL is the standard classification (i.e. CI type) used for an application release. Using classifications helps to reduce the information on screens and reports.

Table 5 – Example configuration status report

CI identifier	CI Type	Name	Version	Status	Changed by	Date	Related change	Related known errors
A0052	APP_REL	Payroll	2.01	Dev	F. Smith	1/1/xx	RFC0645	KE302
								KE303
A0052	APP_REL	Payroll	2.00	Test	J. Patel	2/6/xx	RFC0256	KE201
A0052	APP_REL	Payroll	1.02	Live	D. Keele	6/1/xx	RFC0103	KE085
A0052	APP_REL	Payroll	1.01	Retired	S. Petro	1/9/xx	RFC0056	KE022

Information for other processes

Configuration management reports play an important role in the service provider's planning, decision-making and support activities by the service provider. For example the information in the reports is used by IT staff, customers, projects and suppliers.

An ISO/IEC 20000 auditor may also ask how information on reports from the configuration management process is used by other service management processes. Reports that provide evidence of the integration of the configuration management process with other processes include:

- the latest status of CIs with related documentation and version history;

- a list and status of CIs affected by a change;

- a list and status of problem reports and known errors related to the affected CIs;

- a number of changes for each service, environment or CI type;

- an audit trail of changes made to a CI e.g. changes in the status, location, owner, version;

- a list of CIs at a physical location or business unit (e.g. in preparation for a physical audit);

- a list of software versions in the master software library, versions and status;

- a baseline of the appropriate CIs before a release to the live environment;

- a baseline comparison report e.g. Acceptance test and production, Before and after a change;

- a release comparison report e.g. Application X release 2.1 and 2.2.

An auditor may check that there is a clear description of each configuration management report including its identity, purpose, audience and details of the data source.

The service reporting requirements of ISO/IEC 20000-1, 6.2 also apply to the reports that are produced by the configuration management process. Service reports are described in BIP 0032, *Making metrics work*.

Configuration verification and audit

Scope of the verification and audit

Configuration verification and audit is the activity that reviews CIs to check that the actual CIs match the CIs documented. An objective of a configuration audit is to ensure that software and intellectual property used by the organization is properly licensed and used in accordance with the terms and conditions agreed with the supplier.

The verification and audit activities also check that:

- CIs meet their required attributes and conform to their specification;
- physical configurations are protected and have not been corrupted;
- physical configurations match the details recorded in the CMDB;
- the intellectual capital of the organization is protected;
- the completeness and correctness of the CMDB against the actual physical or electronic CIs;
- the completeness of changed CIs;
- there have been no unauthorized changes.

Many service providers perform audits on samples of CIs. This is a cost effective approach that will be acceptable for an ISO/IEC 20000 audit if the service provider can demonstrate that the sample is statistically sound and is therefore representative of all the CIs that are the subject of the audit.

ISO/IEC 20000-1 requires that audits include the recording of deficiencies, making corrections and reporting on the outcome of the audit. ISO/IEC 20000-2 recommends that nonconformities should be recorded and assessed with corrective action initiated and feedback and input provided to a plan for improving the service.

Verification and audit scheduling

The configuration management process owner is responsible for ensuring that verification and audit activities are scheduled. An audit plan and/or schedule is usually documented in, or referenced from, the overall configuration management plan. Audits are typically carried out to an agreed timetable e.g. before and after major change, after a disaster, and by sampling at random intervals.

ISO/IEC 20000-2 recommends scheduling of both physical and functional audits. Often both types of audit are done at the same time, e.g. before an application release.

An example of the types of configuration audits for software assets is shown in Table 6. In this example the schedule of configuration audits aims to ensure that commercial software assets and the associated licenses are accurate. A rolling audit is scheduled for three locations that are given the abbreviations L1, L2 and L3, across each quarter of the year i.e. Q1, Q2, Q3 and Q4.

Table 6 – Extract from a configuration audit schedule

Audit and frequency	Configuration audit activity	Q1	Q2	Q3	Q4
Software asset verification - Quarterly	Reconciliation between what is installed on each platform and what was authorized for installation, including reporting on exceptions identified	L1 L2 L3	L1 L2 L3	L1 L2 L3	L1 L2 L3
Software licensing compliance - Quarterly	Reconciliation between effective licences owned and licenses required for software used. The bases for and calculations of effective licenses	L1 L2 L3	L1 L2 L3	L1 L2 L3	L1 L2 L3
Software asset verification - 6 monthly	Verification of the inventory of software (originals, definitive master versions, builds and distribution copies)	L1 L2	L3	L1 L2	L3
Hardware and platform verification - 6 monthly	Verification of the hardware and platform inventory including locations	L1 L2	L3	L1 L2	L3
Software asset verification - Annually	Verification of the physical store of proof of license and related contract documentation		L3	L1	L2

Example metrics and audit evidence

The examples shown below are only illustrations as each service provider may meet the requirements of ISO/IEC 20000 by using different metrics.

Table 7- Example metrics

Metric	Type of metric	Purpose and ISO/IEC 20000 objectives
Scope and definition	Percentage of the IT services and configurations identified and accounted for against the configuration management plan targets	To define the components of the service and infrastructure
Compliance	Decrease in the number of non-compliances e.g. software licenses	To define and control the components of the service and infrastructure
Quality of information	Usage of configuration to support the other service management processes, proactive actions and preventative maintenance	Configuration information supports effective service management

Evidence on the effectiveness of a process should not be produced specifically for an audit; evidence should be documents and records used as a normal part of the process.

As a minimum the auditor will expect to see evidence of the effectiveness of how each requirement is met, i.e. evidence that supports how each service provider meets the requirements shown by the use of the verb '**shall**'. Each service provider may have processes and procedures that vary at a detailed level, whilst still meeting the requirements of ISO/IEC 20000-1, so that different audit evidence may be appropriate for different service providers. What evidence is necessary is left to the judgment of the individual auditor but typical examples are illustrated in Table 8.

Table 8 – Example audit evidence for requirements

Objective and requirement	Example audit evidence
Objective: To define and control the components of the service and infrastructure and maintain accurate configuration information.	
To define the components of the service and infrastructure	The structure of the services is reflected in the configuration breakdown structure and CMDB
All configuration items **shall** be uniquely identifiable and recorded in a CMDB to which update access **shall** be strictly controlled. The CMDB **shall** be actively managed and verified to ensure its reliability and accuracy	• Reports from the CMDB are used for configuration audits • Configuration audit reports demonstrate that the CMDB is within required target levels for accuracy
Configuration audit procedures **shall** include the recording of deficiencies, corrective actions and reporting on the outcome	• Deficiencies and nonconformances identified during configuration audits • Reports on the progress of corrective actions

CHAPTER 3

Change management (ISO/IEC 20000-1, 9.2)

Introduction

This chapter describes the key features of the change management process that are necessary for the process to meet the ISO/IEC 20000-1 objective:

'To ensure all changes are assessed, approved, implemented and reviewed in a controlled manner.'

The change management process includes procedures required to identify, review, approve and incorporate change into a managed environment. The ISO/IEC 20000 requirements can be summarized as follows:

- all requests for changes are clearly defined, recorded and classified;

- changes are assessed for their risk, impact and business benefit;

- changes are authorized, approved, checked and implemented in a controlled manner;

- changes are scheduled and coordinated;

- emergency changes are managed;

- unsuccessful changes can be reversed or remedied;

- all changes are reviewed for success and any actions taken after implementation;

- change records are analyzed and improvements input to service improvement planning.

This chapter also includes example metrics and evidence for an ISO/IEC 20000 audit.

What is effective change management?

Effective change management is a process that is responsive to business needs and priorities. Some service providers achieve this by having a single change management process that covers both business changes and IT changes.

The characteristics of an effective change management process are:

* changes are delivered successfully, on time and within budget;

* no unauthorized changes;

* changes are grouped and packaged for efficient implementation;

* changes are planned - there are few unplanned and emergency changes;

* close co-ordination with customers, projects, development and suppliers;

* changes do not cause problems;

* the process is efficient and so does not cause unnecessary delays;

* staff understand the process and can follow it easily;

* only relevant people are involved at each stage of change;

* clear accountability at each stage of managing a change.

To meet the requirements of ISO/IEC 20000, the change management process needs to be integrated with the configuration management process. When the two processes are integrated each time a change is made, accurate information on configurations is available so that the correct CIs and versions are released into the correct environment. As changes are implemented the configuration management information is updated.

An example of a change management process and its relationship to the configuration management process is shown in Figure 8.

Recording changes

ISO/IEC 20000-1 requires all change requests to be recorded. A request for change should identify the CI(s) that will be affected by the change.

Recording all changes ensures that:

* there is a full audit trail of changes;

* change records can be analyzed;

- reporting is useful and consistent;
- all the costs associated with changes are understood e.g. for each service, by customer, by business unit.

The configuration verification and audits in Chapter 2 provide evidence of whether all changes are recorded and controlled by the change management process. The configuration verification and audit stage produces a report of errors in the configuration data or the actual CIs. Unauthorized changes can be identified by using this information. For example the problem management process may identify an unauthorized change after requesting a configuration audit to identify the root cause of failure for:

- downtime;
- a major incident(s);
- an increase in incident volume;
- problems and errors;

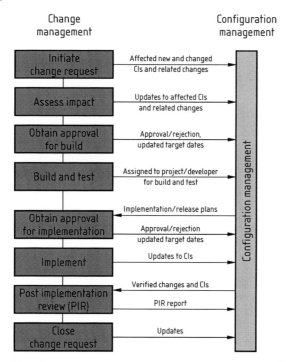

Note: The change management process oversees and coordinates the impact assessment, approval, build, test and implementation of the change.

Figure 8 – Example change management process (normal workflow)

Many service providers have a change management policy that invokes disciplinary action if an unauthorized change is made. An auditor may ask the management team about their role in preventing unauthorized change. Evidence that there is management commitment to preventing unauthorized change may be in the form of records such as those on disciplinary action taken when an unauthorized change has been made. There may be national legislation or an organizational policy that constrains the use of personal information in this way, in which case an auditor would seek alternative evidence of management commitment.

Classifying different types of change

ISO/IEC 20000-1 includes a requirement that all requests for change are classified e.g. urgent, emergency, major, minor.

The classification rules are normally based on several features of the change, such as:

- scale of the change;

- potential impact if the change fails;

- risk that the change will fail;

- benefits of making the change;

- risk and impact if the change is not made.

The classifications can also be linked to features such as the timetable for the change and the person or people who will agree the change, as described below. Classifying the change in this way enables the requests for change to be prioritized and managed easily.

Some of the resistance to the change management process can be avoided by using different procedures for different types of change so that the complexity and overhead of the change process is suitable for each type of change.

This is also much more effective for scheduling. For a small proportion of changes, the defining characteristic is the need to make a change in an emergency. Typical examples of ways to classify changes to allow the efficient processing of each type of change are shown in Table 9.

Table 9 – Example classifications for changes

Typical classification	Description	Examples
Change model or change type	Determines workflow for different types of change	Routine, Normal, Emergency
Risk	Risk to the business and the IT services	High, Medium, Low
Business impact	Impact on the organization. May be combined with change category to determine approval	High, Medium, Low Global, Regional, Country, Site
Priority	Priority to be used in scheduling the change	Critical, High, Medium, Low
Change category/change authority	Determines which people need to be involved with reviewing and approving the RFC	Minor, Significant, Major

Change management lifecycles/models

For greater efficiency, different types of change may follow a different change lifecycle and have different workflows i.e. the classification is used to determine which procedure is used for managing the change, such as the examples shown in Table 10.

For example, an organization may allow low risk 'routine' changes to go through a simple change lifecycle or workflow. When this is the case the method for implementing a routine change is proven. Typically budgetary authority is given in advance, based on a cost agreed in advance.

The routine change is typically something that has been done many times before, is simple, will rarely fail and will have little impact on the service if it does fail.

The manager responsible for changes (often referred to as the change manager) may choose to be informed of these changes, rather than be involved in authorizing each change individually. The change manager is usually responsible for deciding what changes can be implemented as routine changes.

In contrast a normal change has a longer lifecycle than a routine change. This means that the risks and impact of the normal change is given more attention than is given to a routine change.

It is good practice to ensure that the stages of the change lifecycle for each type of change are consistent across the organization. This avoids misunderstandings on who does what and when it is done, which can result in changes failing or changes that conflict when being done at the same time.

Table 10 illustrates some commonly used relationships between type of change and a lifecycle with a series of sequential stages.

Table 10 – Examples of lifecycles for different types of change

Type of change	Example life cycles for CI types
Routine	Raised, Assigned, Closed
Normal	Raised, Impact Assessment, Authorized, Scheduled, Implemented, Reviewed, Closed
Emergency	Raised, Approved, Reviewed, Closed

Emergency changes

It is important to plan in advance for how emergency changes will be managed. By their nature emergency changes are done very quickly, and each normally carries higher risk than if the same change were made following a longer lifecycle, which would provide more time for detailed consideration of each aspect of the change.

Unless emergency changes are planned for, the process may degenerate in to confusion and result in a worsening of the situation.
ISO/IEC 20000-2 recommends that the usual change management process is followed as far as possible for emergency changes. Some steps may be completed later or documented retrospectively e.g. independent testing. It is also common for the same stages to be followed but for each stage to be accelerated.

Because emergency changes will sometimes be necessary and also present a high level of risk, ISO/IEC 20000-1 requires the service provider to have emergency change policies, processes and procedures to control the authorization and implementation of emergency changes. An auditor may ask to see these documents and then check that they have been followed by sampling some emergency change records. An auditor may also check whether the use of the emergency change process complies with the agreed definition of an emergency, or whether the service provider abuses the emergency change process for changes that could have been scheduled in advance.

Roles in change management

One of the challenges that face service providers is understanding which individuals in customer and supplier organizations have what roles, responsibilities, accountabilities and authority levels relating to making changes. This is required by ISO/IEC 20000-1 because best practice change management means all changes are assessed, approved, implemented and reviewed in a controlled manner. Control requires clarity on roles and responsibilities for all changes and for all stages of the change lifecycle. For example, who has the authority to approve each type of change?

An ISO/IEC 20000 audit will check that the service provider has identified and documented stakeholders, customers, users and IT involved in the change management process.

ISO/IEC 20000 does not specify how this should be documented. One method is to obtain this information from the configuration management process as the information about the owner/custodian of affected CIs should be available for each CI or CI type.

Other formats can be used, for example a variation on the responsibility matrices given in BIP 0031, *Why people matter*.

Change initiator

Initiating a request for change is a key interface between change management and customers, projects, developers, suppliers and the other service management processes. It is important that the change initiator has appropriate authority to raise a request for change and sufficient information to clearly define the proposed change.

Change manager

The change manager usually has overall responsibility for the change management process on an operational, day-to-day basis. This person has responsibility for ensuring that the process is established and that the agreed process is followed, including the correct type being chosen for changes and the correct people authorizing each change. This person does not normally actually have any involvement or responsibility for changes actually being made, and may have no responsibility for the actual recording of changes.

This person may also be the change management process owner, as described in Chapter 5. Some service providers separate the responsibility for the process on a day-to-day operational basis from process ownership.

The change manager in a large service provider or one that is making many changes may have a team, often combining the change and configuration management processes.

The typical responsibilities for a change manager include:

- classifying requests for change;
- approving changes that do not need to be approved by the change authority;
- scheduling changes with advice from the change authority;
- overseeing building, testing, implementation and back-out of changes;
- coordinating audits and reviews of changes.

Change administrator

The change manager is often supported by one or more change administrators who are actively involved in the process, normally on a day-to-day operational basis.

Change authority

Formal approval is obtained for each change from people often referred to as the change authority. The change authority may actually be an individual but it is more commonly a role shared by several people.

A group of people who have collective authority for approving changes are often referred to as a Change Advisory Board. Many service providers link authority levels for changes to monetary values such as the estimated cost of the change.

The levels of authorization are linked to the classification of the change, so that for each type a different level of authority applies.

For example, large changes that affect several distributed sites may need to be approved by a higher level change authority such as a global change board or even, in exceptional circumstances, a Board of Directors.

Other change management roles

Typical roles involved in the change management process are:

- Change developer/builder, supplier of the change e.g. project, developer, external supplier;
- Independent tester e.g. a tester that is independent of the Change builder;

- Change implementer, person who implements the change into the environment.

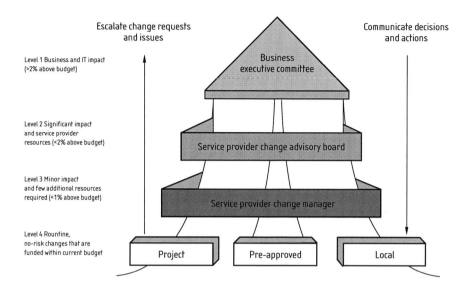

Escalate change requests and issues

Communicate decisions and actions

Level 1 Business and IT impact (>2% above budget)

Level 2 Significant impact and service provider resources (<2% above budget)

Level 3 Minor impact and few additional resources required (<1% above budget)

Level 4 Rountine, no-risk changes that are funded within current budget

Business executive committee

Service provider change advisory board

Service provider change manager

Project | Pre-approved | Local

Figure 9 – Example of a change authorization structure

Defining and recording requests for change

When a change request is raised it is important that good quality information is recorded against a clearly defined service and/or CI. Having an unambiguous link between the change and what the change will affect ensures that the whole process works efficiently. To be effective it is also important that the change request is written in appropriate language for the target audience to understand e.g. business language for customers and technical language for the service provider's own staff.

If a change is badly documented, a reliable impact assessment may not be possible. For example, badly documented changes are unlikely to hold all the information required for an impact assessment, or may hold information that is misleading. Missing or misleading information may result in the impact assessment being based on incorrect assumptions, leading to incorrect conclusions. The result could be a failed change that impacts on the service.

Typical information that is recorded on a change request that will meet the requirements and recommendations of ISO/IEC 20000 are shown in Table 11.

Table 11 – Examples of change request attributes

ISO/IEC 20000 requirement	Attribute example
All requests for change **shall** be recorded Service and infrastructure changes **shall** have a clearly defined and documented scope	• Unique identifier • Description of proposed change • Identity of CIs to be changed including version, build, baseline (possibly added to the record after it is initially raised)
All requests for change **shall** be ….. classified.	• Change type e.g. planned, unplanned, emergency • Category e.g. major, significant, minor • Priority • Urgency Normally all four attributes are used
The scheduled implementation dates of changes **shall** be used as the basis for change and release scheduling	• Scheduled implementation date • Related implementation/release plan
Changes **shall** be approved and then checked and **shall** be implemented in a controlled manner	Audit trail of approvals and updates including status
….. **shall** include the manner in which the change **shall** be reversed or remedied if unsuccessful	Related back-out or remediation plan
All changes **shall** be reviewed for success and any actions taken after implementation	Post implementation review date, comment or report where the policy/process/procedure requires it

Assessing the impact of proposed changes

ISO/IEC 20000-1 requires that all changes are assessed for their risk, impact and business benefit. The configuration management process provides information for impact assessment, such as a list of the potentially affected CIs and the owner or custodian.

The impact analysis will depend on the scale and type of change. The owner of the CI that is to be changed and all affected parties are identified and asked to contribute to an assessment of the impact, the risk of the change and the business benefits.

The detail recorded for an impact assessment depends on the type of change and the assessment technique used. For example, a major change may require a detailed impact assessment to be recorded. In contrast a minor change may be documented by a few sentences in the main body of the change request.

If many people are involved in impact assessment it is usual to summarize the overall views in the body of the change request clearly so staff can understand the impact of the proposed change. The detailed impact assessments would still be available as well.

Many service providers implement an impact assessment procedure based around a standard form or screen so that all aspects of the impact assessment are included.

Budgeting and accounting practices provide the mechanisms for predicting and tracking the costs of a change which is needed to quantify the business benefit of the change.

The change management process owner is responsible for ensuring that the process for impact assessment, including any forms or screens, is suitable for those with the authority to approve changes to be able to make a good management decision. BIP 0038, *Integrated service management* provides examples of impact assessment questions related to ISO/IEC 20000 requirements for assessing the impact of a new or changed service.

Assessing changes in relation to each other

Proposed changes also need to be assessed in relation to one another and against the existing planned schedule of changes. This ensures that the full impact of each change is understood before the change is scheduled avoiding a clash between two separate changes. For example, by looking at the changes that are targeted for a weekend the impact assessment may identify a clash between two changes because of the order or timing. Batching changes also saves effort (and costs).

Scheduling changes

Scheduling is an important activity that enables the service provider to respond to real business needs and demands by planning the implementation of changes that maximize business benefit ahead of other changes.

ISO/IEC 20000-1 requires that the scheduled implementation dates of changes are used as the basis for change and release scheduling. This means that changes that are already scheduled for specific time slots (often called change windows) are not moved unnecessarily. If implementation dates are changed it is important that impact assessment and approval is repeated.

The approved and scheduled changes are typically documented in a plan, schedule or change calendar that is then used in planning further changes and releases.

ISO/IEC 20000-1 requires that the schedule of planned change is communicated to all relevant parties. Many service providers do this by making the plan accessible via the intranet. The internet may be used if suppliers on remote locations are involved.

The advantage of publishing the schedule of planned changes is that those responsible for implementing change requests can try to schedule their changes at times that do not affect other already planned and scheduled changes.

If there are a large number of changes it is usual to breakdown the schedule of planned changes by service and/or geographical area affected.

Some service providers adopt change freezes when the risk of a change, however well managed, is not acceptable, for example, in periods of unusually important business activity, or immediately before a major service or infrastructure change.

Approving or rejecting requests for change

Cultural issues

The culture of a service provider's organization will influence the manner in which changes are approved. Hierarchical structures for authorizing changes may well impose many levels of change approval, while flatter structures may allow a more streamlined approach.

Similarly, the culture of the customer's organization influences the change management process, particularly for organizations that are not pre-disposed to follow standards or processes unless forced to do so.

Some organizations prefer to concentrate authority onto a small number of people, whilst others prefer a large committee structure for decision making.

Whatever approach and criteria are used for the acceptance or rejection of requests for change, an ISO/IEC 20000 auditor may request evidence of the approval process and will assess the effectiveness of this. Evidence of interest to the auditor may be sample requests for change records or minutes of a meeting where the decision was taken e.g. Change Advisory Board minutes.

Staged approval

Many organizations implement several stages of approval, particularly for changes that will ultimately incur significant costs. For example:

- **Stage 1**: resources to assess and define the requirements for a change;
- **Stage 2**: resources to build and test a change (often done as part of a project);
- **Stage 3**: implementation of a change into a controlled environment (e.g. acceptance test or production).

This may be tracked on one or more change requests.

Change authorization

The change authority roles described in the section on *Roles in change management*, considers the business benefits and makes recommendations as to whether the change should be approved for work, approved for implementation or rejected.

Changes that require approval for implementation into the acceptance test or production environment need to have an implementation date and time otherwise the impact cannot be assessed.

Rejected changes

If changes are rejected it is important that the change initiator is notified of the decision and the reason for the decision so that they may reconsider and replan. The role of the change initiator is described in the section on Roles in change management.

Implementation

Pre-implementation checks

ISO/IEC 20000-1 requires that changes are checked before implementation and then implemented in a controlled manner and fully documented. This typically includes:

- checking that authorized changes are properly built and conform to their specification;
- checking that changes to CIs can be verified during implementation;
- ensuring that changes have back-out or remediation plans in case of failure.

Changes are normally implemented by a person in the group that is the owner or custodian for the CI being changed. The change management process is responsible for:

- coordinating the implementation of changes;

- liaising with configuration and release management as appropriate;

- ensuring that there are records with evidence of verification of the change;

- coordinating the 'back-out' or remediation of failed changes.

Verification

The change management process checks that the change is implemented in a controlled manner by checking that the change records and configuration documentation are accurate and complete. This may include checking that the change record is correctly linked to the affected CIs, and the correct version of the implementation and release documentation is issued.

If required the change management process may request a configuration verification and audit of the related CIs from the configuration management process.

Review and closure

ISO/IEC 20000-1 requires that all changes are reviewed for success, and that any actions are taken after implementation. Different types of change typically require different levels of review.

For some changes, such as a major change, a post-implementation review meeting will be held to review the outcomes. A post-implementation review aims to check that the change met its objectives, that customers are happy with the results and that there have been no unexpected side-effects. It is good practice to record lessons learned and feed any improvements into the service improvement programme. The outcomes and actions are reported in the meeting minutes.

For other changes a summary of a review may be recorded on the change record or a related document e.g. showing the impact of a change on the number of incidents and problems for the affected CI in the period after the change.

ISO/IEC 20000-2 recommends that the change management process should review all completed emergency changes to:

- check that by-passed steps have been completed;

- check that the documentation is complete;

- verify that the change was a true emergency.

The actual costs, resources and time are usually recorded as part of the review and closure activities.

The change records are closed when all the documentation has been completed.

Analyzing changes and inputs to service improvement

A proactive aspect of the change management process is the analysis of changes to identify trends and opportunities for process improvement. ISO/IEC 20000-1 requires change records to be analyzed regularly to detect increasing levels of changes, frequently recurring types, emerging trends and other relevant information. The results and conclusions of the analysis need to be recorded to meet the requirements of ISO/IEC 20000-1.

The change management process owner is responsible for scheduling regular analyses and ensuring that the results and conclusions are recorded.

Typical examples are:

- increase in volume of changes by CI type and/or owner;

- variation in actual vs. estimated cost/resource/time;

- volume and frequency of changes against success over time;

- maximum/average/minimum time for each step in the workflow by type and/or category of change.

All processes in service management and the PDCA cycle place a high level of importance on continual improvements to the quality of the service. An auditor will expect to see evidence of the information from the analyses, results and conclusions to be used in planning service improvements.

Example metrics and audit evidence

As described in Chapter 2, a definitive list of metrics and audit evidence for this process is not possible and those given in Table 12 and 13 are illustrations only.

Table 12 – Example metrics

Metric	Type of metric	Purpose and ISO/IEC 20000 objectives
Quality	Number of successful changes (e.g. benefits within time, within budget) Number of unsuccessful changes (by root cause) Percentage variance from estimated cost of change Number of unauthorized changes Number and per cent of unplanned/emergency changes	To ensure all changes are assessed, approved, implemented and reviewed in a controlled manner
Efficiency	Resources spent on work required when reversing or remedying unsuccessful changes and releases	The service is deliverable and manageable at the right cost
Cost	Cost per change (by resource, asset type, etc.)	The service is deliverable and manageable at the right cost

Table 13 – Example audit evidence

Objective and requirement	Example audit evidence
Objective: To ensure all changes are assessed, approved, implemented and reviewed in a controlled manner.	
All changes **shall** be assessed, approved, implemented and reviewed in a controlled manner	• All requests for change have been correctly recorded, classified, assessed and actioned • Change documentation is up-to-date and complete • Associated CIs have been updated • Unauthorized changes are reported
Changes **shall** be approved in accordance with the change management policies and procedures	• Approvals records are complete and authorized by the right person or group
Change records **shall** be analysed regularly	• Regular trend reports e.g. showing the number of changes of each type of change against the success criteria

CHAPTER 4

Release management
(ISO/IEC 20000-1, 10.1)

Introduction

This chapter describes the key features of the release management process required so that the process delivers the ISO/IEC 20000-1 objective:

'To deliver, distribute and track one or more changes in a release into the live environment.'

The process is used to implement a group of related and compatible CIs in a batch, known as a release. Typically this means a group of changes are made to a set of CIs using a consistent repeatable method.

Typical circumstances where the release management process is the most advantageous approach are as follows:

- changes to a desktop build (hardware and software);

- desktop application applied across many PCs;

- release of a new or changed service to many users;

- a maintenance package of fixes or repairs;

- application release;

- major upgrade such as a technology refresh;

- platform update such as a security patch.

Each release is governed by a request for change raised via the change management process. This ensures that the group of changes in a release are authorized, scheduled and implemented correctly.

The release management process also ensures that the groups of changes in each release are compatible with each other and that none clash with other unrelated changes.

The requirements can be summarized as follows:

- a release policy is agreed with the business and all relevant parties;

- releases and roll outs are planned well in advance;

- all releases are tested in a controlled acceptance test environment prior to distribution;

- resources are coordinated during release and roll out;

- release mechanisms ensure the integrity of components during each stage of:

  - installation;

  - handling;

  - packaging; and

  - delivery;

- unsuccessful releases can be backed-out or remedied;

- the success and failure of releases is measured;

- provision of inputs to service improvement.

What is effective release management?

A holistic approach

Although many service providers have teams that operate in silos or processes that are not integrated, this is not acceptable for a service provider aiming to achieve ISO/IEC 20000. For example, the release management process must be closely integrated with configuration and change management. The release management process works with many parties crossing organizational boundaries, and it is important to define the scope of release management

The importance of integration is also linked to the need for the release management process to have a holistic view of change to a service or to the infrastructure. A holistic view ensures that all aspects of a release are considered together, both technical and non-technical.

Careful planning of releases ensures that there is no ambiguity about what tasks are included in the release management process, what tasks are included in other processes and how processes interface to any projects that are providing a release.

Many suppliers and the business deliver a release across a distributed environment. This leads to better alignment of services with the business needs as releases are scheduled at times to suit the business.

All changes and CIs in a release are tracked via interfaces to the change and configuration management processes. This level of control also helps the service provider achieve compliance with legal, regulatory and contractual requirements related to managing intellectual property rights and software licensing. Figure 1 in Chapter 1 shows the relationships between release, change and configuration management.

Optimizing a release

Many changes may be grouped into one release and may be designed, tested and released together if the amount of change involved can be handled by the business, the service provider and its customers. However, if many independent changes are grouped into a release then this may create unnecessary dependencies that are difficult to manage. If not enough changes are grouped into a release then the overhead of managing more releases can be time consuming and waste resources.

The release management process can provide benefits such as significant cost savings and better control. This is often achieved by:

- grouping related changes into a release for efficient implementation;

- standardizing the release activities;

- automating the release process (once there is a standard method);

- removing unnecessary approval steps and handoffs;

- reducing manual actions that cause errors and inconsistencies;

- changing the frequency of releases to maximize resource utilization.

Effective release management results in:

- no waiting time or re-work;

- few back-outs;

- a successful roll out across the user base on time and to budget;

- cheaper and streamlined process that all parties understand;

- all CIs involved in a release are traceable and auditable.

Stages of the release management process

As shown in Figure 10, within the release management process there are the release process and the roll out process. These cover the three main aspects of the release management process, which are:

- planning;

- ensuring that a release is developed according to the customer and service providers needs;

- rolling out the release to target business units, users, and platforms.

In many service providers, the release management process is closely linked with projects, such as the work of a development team producing releases. Sometimes the team responsible for the release management process works in isolation as a consequence. This isolation is bad practice, and can cause issues for the service provider.

The release management process should instead provide an independent and well integrated interface between the rest of the service management processes and the source of the releases. This is the case irrespective of whether the team involved in implementing the release is part of the project team producing the release or part of the 'service management team'. The best practices specified for the release management process are independent of the organizational form adopted by the service provider.

The best practice integrated approach required by ISO/IEC 20000 ensures that a release:

- complies with the appropriate standards;

- meets the requirements of the business;

- meets the service provider's requirements;

- addresses operational issues;

- is rolled out with suitable notice to those involved or affected, such as operational teams.

The release management process must also ensure that information on any operational issues and known errors is passed on to the team that produced the release, so that these can be addressed, managed and corrected. In some cases the error is not corrected and is instead treated as a known error. This is described in BIP 0037, *Keeping the service going.*

The release policy determines how the release is planned and defined, and is the first stage of the release process. This is then followed through to the acceptance test stage. At this point the roll out process starts with planning of the actual roll out. The roll out process continues to the point at which the release is reviewed.

At all stages the release management process is integrated with the change and configuration management processes, ensuring that there is flow of information to the release management process and that updates are fed back to the change and configuration management processes.

The release process also interfaces to the source of the release. In Figure 10 the example used is the development lifecycle.

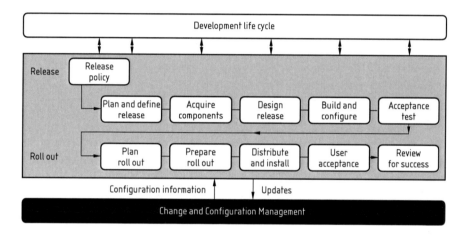

Figure 10 – Example of release and roll out

Release policy

A release policy helps to set expectations on the nature of a release and when a release will be more appropriate than a series of separate changes.

To meet the requirements in ISO/IEC 20000 a release policy needs to state the frequency and type of releases.

In addition ISO/IEC 20000-2 recommends that the following are included in the policy:

- roles and responsibilities for release management;

- the authority for the release to go into acceptance test and production environments;

- rules for unique identification and description of all releases;

- approach to grouping changes into a release;
- an agreed approach to automating in order to aid repeatability and efficiency, covering:
  - build;
  - installation;
  - release distribution process.
- rules on verification and acceptance of a release.

The role of release manager

Understanding the release policy means that all those involved in a release are also able to plan and budget for resources well in advance. It is therefore essential that someone with sufficient authority and responsibility for the release management process works with an equivalent manager involved in the service level management process. They are required to define the approach and agree this with the relevant parties, such as the customer.

The managers who need to work closely together have roles that are commonly referred to as the 'release manager' and the 'service level manager'.

A typical release manager is actively involved in the process, normally on a day-to-day operational basis. This usually includes ensuring that the agreed process is followed and that records and plans are updated in the correct timescales and with the correct information.

Some service providers choose to combine the role of the operational release manager and the release management process owner, as described in BIP 38, *Integrated service management*.

Other roles involved in release management

There are often many other roles involved in release and roll out management, and it is therefore important to ensure that the accountabilities and responsibilities for all stages are clear as the release and its constituent CIs move from the development lifecycle and into the production environment.

The configuration management process assists with this by documenting the scope of the release management roles, accountabilities and responsibilities for each CI type through release cycle. This is described in more detail in Chapter 2.

Configuration Item Type	Development			Pre-Acceptance Test	Acceptance Test	Acceptance Test	Live
	Released from		from	Released from	Accepted by	Released from	Accepted and supported by
Central application	Development manager			Configuration manager	Test manager	Configuration management	Operations and support manager
Database schema	Development manager			Development manager	Database administrator	Configuration management	Database administrator
Physical database	Development manager			Development manager	Database administrator	Configuration management	Database administrator
Central application environment	Environment manager			Environment manager	Operations and support manager	Configuration management	Operations and support manager
Internet	Development manager			Environment manager	Web master	Configuration management	Web master
Personal computers	Logistics			Environment manager	Desktop support	Configuration management	Desktop support
Desktop build-new release	Development manager			Configuration manager	Desktop support	Configuration management	Desktop support
Desktop installation	Environment manager			Environment manager	Desktop support	Configuration management	Desktop support
Release authorization	Development configuration manager			Development configuration manager	Test manager	As stated in release policy and approved by change management	Business operations and IT service desk

Figure 11 – Roles and Responsibilities for a release

Frequency of releases

The release policy assists all those involved or affected to plan their resources. Different parts of the customer's business may have very different needs, each needing to be managed individually and carefully. For example, a marketing department may require a release of every day whereas a financial department may prefer to have a release every quarter.

The policy, process and procedures for release management also need to cater for emergency releases.

Some service providers find that reducing the frequency of releases can reduce disruption to the live services significantly, and also reduce overheads associated with managing releases. However, this may not be acceptable to fast moving businesses where speed-to-market is essential and the business requires daily updates.

There can be a significant impact on the customer's business, service provider and suppliers if the frequency of releases is inappropriate. Working closely with the service level management process minimizes the risk of inappropriate frequency being used.

Release and roll out planning

Planning will depend on the type of release being developed and rolled out as well as the target audience or platforms. For example the planning activities will be different for each of the following types of release:

- new service to target business units, customers, users, platforms;

- desktop release to target computers and users;

- mainframe application to target business units, customers, users;

- security patch by platform.

Agreeing an approach

Good planning and management are essential to package and successfully distribute a release. The approach for each type of release needs to be agreed with the business.

Figure 12 shows two options.

- **Option A** is to perform consecutive releases with all users upgraded at once.

- **Option B** includes a pilot roll out before the full roll out to all users.

Option B also starts the planning for the next release once the previous release is in pilot. This provides the opportunity for more releases a year.

Option A

Release 1.0				Release 1.1			
Plan release	Develop release	Acceptance test	Roll out	Plan release	Develop release	Acceptance test	Roll out

Option B

Release 1.0				
Plan release	Develop release	Acceptance test	Pilot roll out	Full roll out

Release 1.1				
Plan release	Develop release	Acceptance test	Pilot roll out	Full roll out

| Jan | Feb | Mar | Apr | May | Jun | Jul | Aug |

Figure 12 – Examples of release approaches

In distributed environments it is often lower risk to pilot a release at a few locations before rolling out an application e.g. in one country before roll out is done globally. It is also common practice to freeze the contents of a release at a fixed interval before the release is implemented.

ISO/IEC 20000-2 recommends that the release and roll out should be planned in stages as details. This allows the plan to be developed as more information is obtained on the release, providing a better understanding of the most appropriate way of releasing and rolling out. For example if a detailed roll out plan is developed 9 months in advance there are likely to be differences to the contents, the environment that will receive the release and, in particular, the customers business needs.

Release definition

ISO/IEC 20000-1 requires the release documentation to record the:

*   the release deliverables;

*   the release dates;

*   related change requests that are to be implemented;

*   known errors that are fixed;

*   new known errors or problems in the new release.

Figure 13 provides an example of some of the records and relationships between the records used in planning a release. A good configuration management system will help the service provider to keep track of these relationships.

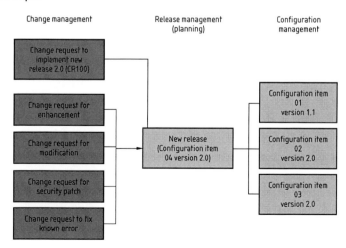

Figure 13 – Defining a release during release planning

Figure 13 shows the records that are created to track the change requests for a new release and the related CIs. Release planning involves reaching agreement on change requests that will be incorporated into the new release (configuration item 04). This new release is approved through the change management process using change request CR100. The new versions of the CI that are to be included in the release are related to the CI for the new release of version 2.0. Configuration management provides reports and information about these documents and the relationships between them as well as the status of each change request and CI.

Release management may use the configuration management verification and audit process to check key criteria for the release definition are met, for example:

- the release is scoped and clearly defined;
- relevant business objectives, policies, requirements and plans are identified;
- the service requirements are clear, unambiguous and can be tested/measured;
- the expected outcomes from operating a new service are expressed in measurable terms and can be measured.

Release and roll out planning

Figure 14 provides a simple example of a high level release and roll out plan that can be used to set the expectations of all parties involved in a release.

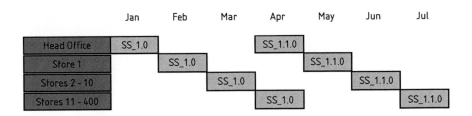

Figure 14 – Example of a release and roll out plan

At a more detailed level it is best practice for the release and roll out plans for the same type of release to contain the same basic activities each time. This makes it easier for service provider staff to repeat the activities consistently for each release.

Approval and communicating the release and roll out plans

ISO/IEC 20000 requires that the plans to roll out a release are agreed and authorized by all relevant parties such as customers, users, operations and support staff. This can be achieved by raising a change request for the release and ensuring that all relevant parties will be informed of the change as a result.

Plans must be communicated to incident management staff as this helps them to prepare for the release and to handle incidents when the release goes live e.g. training staff just before a release will ensure that they can answer the queries when the release is made.

Developing or acquiring software

ISO/IEC 20000-2 recommends that software releases from in-house teams, systems builders, system integrators or other organizations should be verified on receipt, using the configuration verification and audit. It is important that any software versions and other electronic files are stored in configuration management and the relevant secure library.

Designing, building and configuring a release

To meet the ISO/IEC 20000-1 requirements for successful release management, the release and distribution mechanisms need to be carefully designed to ensure that the integrity of hardware and software is protected during installation, handling, packaging and delivery.

In order to achieve these requirements it is best practice to:

- use standard release management procedures and tools;

- reduce manual steps that are error prone and costly;

- ensure that software licences can be managed and authorized;

- ensure that software licences will be re-deployed where appropriate;

- design a release so that it can be backed out or remedied if unsuccessful;

- use software libraries and related repositories to manage and control components during the build and release process;

- enable verification that the target platform satisfies prerequisites before installation;

- enable verification so that a release can be checked for completeness when it reaches its destination;

- check that the build of the release complies with the architecture and all relevant standards.

ISO/IEC 20000-1 includes neither requirements nor recommendations for automation of distribution tools. However, some form of automation is normally beneficial as, when properly used, it can reduce both costs and the risks of a mistake being made.

Acceptance test environment

ISO/IEC 20000-1 requires the service provider to establish a controlled acceptance test environment to build and test all releases prior to distribution into production. This is an all encompassing requirement that the service provider will need to prove to the auditor. The type of evidence that an auditor may seek is:

- configuration baseline report of the acceptance test environment;

- configuration baseline report of the production environment prior to release;

- comparison of the acceptance test environment baseline compared to the production environment, with the differences and how these are to be managed;

- configuration baseline report of the production environment after the release.

However, the acceptance test environment does not need to be a dedicated physical environment. For example, one service provider had no acceptance test environment but did have a maintenance window that allowed enough time to use the production server for the acceptance test prior to installing the release. This may be acceptable as long as there is a well tested back-out or remediation plan should there be any issues.

Release verification

The change management process requirements given in ISO/IEC 20000-1, 9.2 require that new or changed services are accepted by all relevant parties e.g. the customer, stakeholders, service provider staff and suppliers. It is important to base formal approval on the results of the acceptance test. Proactive service providers will ensure that the release requirements are addressed during the design and development of the release as shown in Table 14.

Configuration items for a release

ISO/IEC 20000-2 recommends that all associated updates to documentation should be included in the release e.g. business processes, support documents and service level agreements.

Additional examples of CIs and documentation that would be under configuration management at the acceptance test and release-to-live are:

- release definition and requirements to enable changes to be made against these in the future;

- environment configuration baseline e.g. acceptance test;

- application configuration baseline and release;

- training plan for service management, support staff and customers;

- communications plan(s);

- test plans;

- back-out/remediation and contingency plans;

- service management documentation (if new or changed service);

- support documentation e.g. support procedures, diagnostic aids, operating and administration instructions;

- build, release, installation and distribution processes and procedures;

- known error list;

- release note(s);

- evidence of acceptance testing;

- evidence that the release is ready for release to live.

Table 14 provides examples of acceptance checks that a service provider may perform at the design and acceptance stages when implementing a release (using configuration management verification and audit procedures).

Table 14 – Examples of Release Acceptance Criteria

Release Stage: Design
• The release is clearly scoped and the service management requirements are met by the proposed design
• The service management requirements can be delivered by the proposed design e.g. capacity requirements, availability and performance target
• The service is designed to meet the service providers policies, and service management plans
• The design conforms with the organization's systems architecture, service management and infrastructure standards
• The proposed release design enables the service to be delivered at the estimated cost
• Applications are designed to meet the organization's software licensing policies and constraints
• The design of the service reports complies with the requirements of the IT performance management and service reporting system
• The proposed build and release mechanisms for deployment are efficient and effective e.g. automated and efficient
• The proposed changes to processes that interface with the release management process have been signed off e.g. business relationship management, service level management
• The acceptance test plan tests the requirements and design criteria
• The acceptance test criteria can be tested
• Training plans are develop for service provider staff and users

Table 14 – Examples of Release Acceptance Criteria (*continued*)

Stage: Before acceptance test
• The communications plan for the release ensures all parties involved in acceptance testing are informed about the release
• Training is planned and for staff and users to be involved in acceptance testing
• Sufficient support resources have been planned for the acceptance test, including relevant service management process owners
• All service and infrastructure documentation is under configuration management e.g. service requirements specification
• The CMBD, supporting systems, tools have been updated

Stage: Before implementation into live
• The acceptance test report provides evidence that the acceptance test is completed
• Release documentation is complete and under configuration management
• Roll out plan(s) are accepted by all relevant parties (if applicable)
• The communications plan for the release ensures all parties are informed about the release
• Staff and users are trained and ready
• Sufficient support resources have been planned (link to capacity management)
• All release deliverables are under configuration management e.g. service catalogue, agreements, contracts
• The CMDB, supporting systems and tools have been updated
• The incident and problem management data has been updated

Roll out, distribution and installation

Having established plans for agreeing how and when the roll out of the release is to occur, ISO/IEC 20000-1 includes a requirement that the release is distributed in a way that the integrity of hardware and software is maintained during installation, handling, packaging and delivery.

The details of how this is achieved are often dependent on:

- the type and size of the customer's business activities;

- the number of users/locations (and time zones);

- system type and size;

- other releases or changes that are also occurring;

- the quality and currency of configuration management information;

- the availability (or otherwise) of tools for the automation of the process.

Updating configuration management information

Clause 10.1 of ISO/IEC 20000-1 requires that the release management process includes the updates to configuration information throughout the release process as shown in Figure 15.

As a release is implemented any new versions and CIs are also related to CI for the new release. An audit trail of all changes to CIs and the new release CI is recorded in the CMDB.

During the release process the definitive versions of the software and documentation for the release 1.0 are copied from the 'Definitive Library 01' into the 'Development' environment to implement the changes. 'Development' requests a copy of the definitive release through the CMDB and takes a copy of the definitive versions of the CIs from release R1.0 to develop into versions for release R1.1. When R1.1 has been successfully tested in the pre-acceptance test environment, the CMDB is updated and a definitive copy of the release is placed in the 'Definitive Library 01' ready for release to 'Acceptance Test'. When R1.1 has passed the acceptance tests, the status is updated in the CMDB. As R1.1 is rolled out the CMDB is updated with the details of the installed configuration.

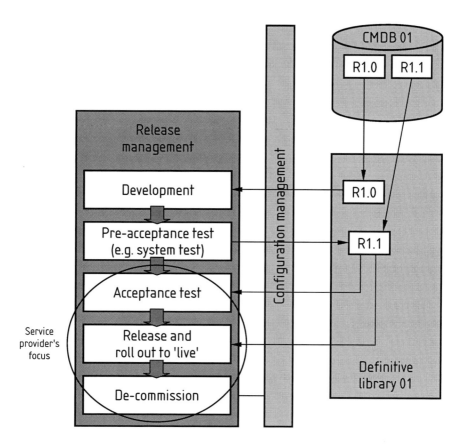

Figure 15 – Updating configuration information during a release

Post release and roll out

ISO/IEC 20000-1 requires the service provider to measure the success and failure of releases by measuring the incidents related to a release in the period following a release. Examples of the type of report that can be used for this are given in BIP 0032, *Making metrics work*.

It is also a requirement that there is an analysis of the impact on the business, IT operations and support staff resources. This is typically input into the post implementation review of the release or associated change.

ISO/IEC 20000-2 recommends that feedback on the release and roll out should be fed back to the post implementation review for the corresponding change request.

ISO/IEC 20000-1 requires that any improvements should also provide input to service improvement planning such as fixes for the next release.

Example metrics and audit evidence

As described in Chapter 2, a definitive list of metrics and audit evidence for this process is not possible and those given in Tables 15 and 16 are illustrations only.

Table 15 – Example metrics

Metric	Type of metric	Purpose and ISO/IEC 20000 objectives
Quality	100% deployment to target users/platforms	To deliver, distribute and track one or more changes in a release into the live environment
Efficiency	Number and percentage deployed with no manual intervention	Release and distribution shall be designed and implemented so that the integrity of hardware and software is maintained during installation, handling, packaging and delivery
Effectiveness	Number and percentage deployed with no errors	
Non-conformance	Number of incidents, problems and known errors identified against the release	Success and failure of releases shall be measured. Measurements shall include incidents related to a release in the period following a release

Table 16 – Example audit evidence for requirements

Objective and requirement	Example audit evidence
Objective: To deliver, distribute and track one or more changes in a release into the live environment.	
The service provider **shall** plan with the business the release of services, systems, software and hardware	• Release plan signed off by the business
	• Releases are delivered to the release plan
Plans .... **shall** be communicated to incident management	• Incident management understand what releases are planned
A controlled acceptance test environment **shall** be established to build and test all releases prior to distribution	• There is a record of the acceptance test environment used to test a release e.g. configuration baseline of the acceptance test environment
	• There is evidence that releases are tested prior to distribution

CHAPTER 5

Management system requirements

This chapter briefly describes the ISO/IEC 20000 requirements of management, including an effective Plan-Do-Check-Act (PDCA) cycle. More details are provided in BIP 0038, *Integrated service management.*

Management Responsibilities

Accountability and responsibility

By meeting the ISO/IEC 20000 requirements the service provider will have clarity on accountability and responsibility for the CIs within the scope of service management. For example, in the:

- **configuration management process**, define accountabilities and responsibilities for managing every CI and providing an audit trail of changes to CIs;

- **change management process**, ensure that authorization levels required to approve changes to a CI are unambiguous, avoiding changes being made without the correct process being followed and therefore presenting less risk to the service and to the customer;

- **release management process**, ensure that whoever is responsible and accountable for each component of the service and for each stage of each release is clear, however many groups are involved across the full lifecycle of the release.

Senior responsible owner

Both parts of ISO/IEC 20000 refer to the appointment of a 'senior responsible owner'. This role is particularly important in contributing to satisfying the regulatory, legal or corporate governance requirements. This is particularly closely linked to the service provider's control and release processes, by which changes are made.

ISO/IEC 20000-2 also recommends that decision-making group with the authority to agree and enforce policies support the senior responsible owner. This decision-making group is often responsible for approving significant changes to the service and infrastructure in the change management process.

Process owner

Process ownership is required for best practice processes. To achieve the ISO/IEC 20000 requirements for active involvement and leadership process owners should be at a level senior enough for the process owner to be able to exert influence and provide leadership for the improvements. The process owner ensures the processes are integrated, which involves cooperating with other process owners.

Many service providers have a central function responsible for the change and configuration management processes and the control activities in release management. This team is often independent of the development and service delivery organization and may be responsible for change, configuration and release management across the systems development lifecycle. The process owner for change and configuration management may be the manager of this team.

Policies, processes and procedures

As described in BIP 0038, *Integrated service management*, the relationship between policy, process and procedure is important, with policies providing management direction which is supported by the processes and procedures, as shown in Figure 16.

Definition: Policy, process and procedure

- **'Policy'** describes the overall intentions and direction of a service provider and is formally expressed by senior management. Policies should be underpinned by processes.

- **'Process'** describes an activity using resources to transform inputs to outputs. Often, the output from one process will directly form the input into the next process. Where this is the case, the processes are integrated, can be managed properly and will be more effective overall.

- **'Procedure'** describes the specified way of carrying out a process; a procedure underpins a process.

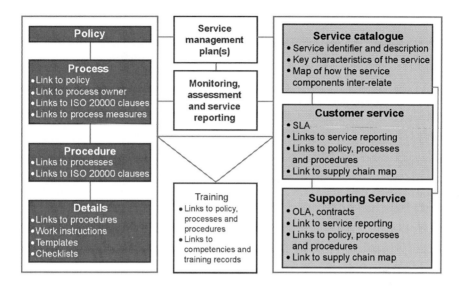

Figure 16 – Service management framework and enabling change

Service management policies are a requirement of ISO/IEC 20000-1. During an ISO/IEC 20000 audit, evidence on the effectiveness of policies will be required. Typical examples for policies for the processes in this book are:

- 'No unauthorized change.......';

- 'Downtime and incidents caused by change will be reviewed and input to the service improvement programme ....';

- 'All changes to CIs are fully and accurately recorded......';

- 'Major releases will be scheduled once per quarter, minor once per month....';

The processes in this book enable the service provider to manage changes to the service management documentation shown in Figure 16. As the management team depends on quality information to make good decisions on changes and improvements, it is important that the impact of change to the documentation are properly assessed and managed.

Plan-Do-Check-Act (PDCA)

The processes in this publication enable any changes to the inputs to 'Manage Services' to be managed to achieve the successful outputs shown in Figure 17.

The change management process is fundamental in ensuring that changes to the inputs shown in Figure 16 are defined, assessed, authorized, planned and implemented in a controlled and timely manner. The post implementation review of such changes is also managed through change management.

Configuration management provides the audit trail of changes to the CIs affected by the PDCA cycle. In addition to the normal process reviews and audits, the verification and audit activities that are part of the configuration management process described in Chapter 2 provide key inputs to service improvement plans. For example, an audit of CIs may discover a discrepancy in the physical infrastructure compared to the configuration management database. This may be due to a process deficiency that needs to be resolved such as an unauthorized change.

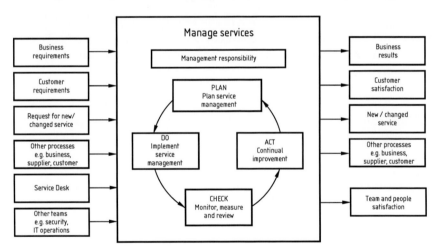

Figure 17 – PDCA cycle and enabling change

Service improvement for enabling change

Service providers achieve significant improvements by improving their change, configuration and release management processes. As the processes are so closely inter-related, they are often reviewed together and service improvements planned and managed together.

Other service management process

Effective integration of processes is fundamental to service management. Other service management processes will be affected by changes, and there are requirements throughout ISO/IEC 20000-1 to manage process changes through the change management process, as described in Chapter 3. Other processes will also have responsibilities for managing CIs. Relationships are described in more detail in BIP 0038, *Integrated service management.*

Planning and implementing new and changed services

Clause 5 of ISO/IEC 20000-1 includes requirements for planning and implementing new or changed services. Although all changes are managed through the change, configuration and release management processes, this clause has specific requirements for managing changes that may impact the scope, requirements, cost and quality of the existing services.

Typical examples of such changes are:

- introduction of a new service e.g. acquisitions, mergers, transfer;

- major change to an existing service;

- new application implemented;

- major extension to the scope of he infrastructure;

- closure of a service.

The requirements of Clause 5 are described in BIP 0038, *Integrated service management.*

APPENDIX A

ISO/IEC 20000 requirements in summary

It is important to refer to ISO/IEC 20000-1 and ISO/IEC 20000-2 and not rely on the abstract given in Tables A.1, A.2 and A.3, which covers only those parts of the ISO/IEC 20000 that are particularly relevant to the three processes in the scope of this book.

Other publications in the 'Achieving ISO/IEC 20000' series feature similar tables covering other requirements in the same way.

Each requirement (signified by the use of the verb '**shall**') is supplemented by informative commentary based on the details in ISO/IEC 20000-2 and related publications (see Appendix B).

Table A.1 – ISO/IEC 20000 requirements with informative commentary/guidance for capacity management

ISO/IEC 20000-1 requirements	ISO/IEC 20000-2 recommendations (*italics*) and additional commentary (**bold**)

Clause 9.1 – Configuration Management

Objective: To define and control the components of the service and infrastructure and maintain accurate configuration information

There **shall** be an integrated approach to change and configuration management planning.	***Configuration management planning and implementation*** *Configuration management **should** be planned and implemented with change and release management to ensure that the service provider can manage its IT assets and configurations effectively.* *Accurate configuration information **should** be available to support the planning and control of changes as new and updated services and systems are released and distributed. The result **should** be an efficient system that integrates the service provider's configuration information processes and those of its customers and suppliers, where appropriate.* *All major assets and configurations **should** be accounted for and have a responsible manager who ensures that appropriate protection and control is maintained, e.g. changes are authorized before implementation.* *Responsibility for implementing controls may be delegated but accountability **should** remain with the responsible manager.* *The responsible manager **should** be provided with the information necessary to discharge this responsibility, e.g. the person authorizing a change may require information on the cost, risks, impact of the change and resources for implementation.* *The infrastructure and/or services **should** have up-to-date configuration management plan(s) that may be stand-alone or form part of other planning documents.*

ISO/IEC 20000-1 requirements	ISO/IEC 20000-2 recommendations (*italics*) and additional commentary (**bold**)
	*They **should** include or describe:* *a) scope, objectives, policies, standards roles and responsibilities;* *b) the configuration management processes to define the configuration items in the service(s) and infrastructure, control changes to the configurations, recording and reporting the status of configuration items and verifying the completeness and correctness of configuration items.* *c) the requirements for accountability, traceability, auditability, e.g. for security, legal, regulatory or business purposes;* *d) configuration control (access, protection, version, build, release controls);* *e) interface control process for identifying, recording, and managing the configuration items and information at the common boundary of two or more organizations, e.g. system interfaces, releases;* *f) planning and establishing the resources to bring assets and configurations under control and maintain the configuration management system, e.g. training;* *g) management of suppliers and sub-contractors performing configuration management.* *NOTE An appropriate level of automation **should** be implemented to ensure that processes do not become either inefficient, error prone or may not be followed at all.*
The service provider **shall** define the interface to financial asset accounting processes. NOTE 1 Financial asset accounting falls outside the scope of this section.	

ISO/IEC 20000-1 requirements

There **shall** be a policy on what is defined as a configuration item and its constituent components.

The information to be recorded for each item **shall** be defined and **shall** include the relationships and documentation necessary for effective service management.

Configuration management **shall** provide the mechanisms for identifying, controlling and tracking versions of identifiable components of the service and infrastructure.

It **shall** be ensured that the degree of control is sufficient to meet the business needs, risks of failure and service criticality.

ISO/IEC 20000-2 recommendations (*italics*) and additional commentary (**bold**)

Configuration identification

All major assets and configurations should be accounted for and have a responsible manager who ensures that appropriate protection and control is maintained

All configuration items **should** *be uniquely identified and defined by attributes that describe their functional and physical characteristics. Information* **should** *be relevant and auditable.*

Appropriate markings, or other methods of identification, **should** *be used and recorded in the configuration management database. Items to be managed* **should** *be identified using established selection criteria and* **should** *include:*

a) all issues and releases of information systems and software (including third-party software) and related system documentation, e.g. requirements specifications, designs, test reports, release documentation;

b) configuration baselines or build statements for each applicable environment, standard hardware builds and release;

c) master hardcopy and electronic libraries, e.g. definitive software library;

d) configuration management package or tools used;

e) licences;

f) security components, e.g. firewalls;

g) physical assets that need to be tracked for financial asset management or business reasons, e.g. secure magnetic media, equipment;

h) service related documentation, e.g. SLAs, procedures;

i) service supporting facilities, e.g. power to computer room;

ISO/IEC 20000-2 recommendations (*italics*) and additional commentary (**bold**)

j) relationships and dependencies between configuration items.

NOTE: Other items that may be considered as configuration items include:

a) other documentation;

b) other assets;

c) other facilities, e.g. site;

d) business units;

e) people.

Appropriate relationships and dependencies between configuration items **should** *be identified to provide the necessary level of control.*

Where traceability is required the process **should** *ensure that configuration items can be traced through the full lifecycle, from requirements documents through to release records, e.g. using a traceability matrix.*

Configuration control

The process **should** *ensure that only authorized and identifiable configuration items are accepted and recorded from receipt to disposal.*

No configuration item **should** *be added, modified, replaced or removed/withdrawn without appropriate controlling documentation, e.g. approved change request, updated release information.*

ISO/IEC 20000-1 requirements

Configuration management **shall** provide information to the change management process on the impact of a requested change on the service and infrastructure configurations.

Changes to configuration items **shall** be traceable and auditable where appropriate, e.g. for changes and movements of software and hardware.

Configuration control procedures **shall** ensure that the integrity of systems, services and service components are maintained.

A baseline of the appropriate configuration items **shall** be taken before a release to the live environment.

85

ISO/IEC 20000-2 recommendations (*italics*) and additional commentary (**bold**)

To protect the integrity of systems, services and the infrastructure, configuration items **should** *be held in a suitable and secure environment which:*

a) protects them from unauthorized access, change or corruption, e.g. virus;

b) provides a means for disaster recovery;

c) permits the controlled retrieval of a copy of the controlled master, e.g. software.

Configuration status accounting and reporting

Current and accurate configuration records **should** *be maintained to reflect changes in the status, location and versions of configuration items.*

Status accounting **should** *provide information on the current and historical data concerned with each configuration item throughout its lifecycle. It* **should** *enable changes to configuration items to be tracked through various states, e.g. ordered, received, in acceptance test, live, under change, withdrawn, disposed.*

Configuration information **should** *be kept current and made available for planning, decision making and managing changes to the defined configurations.*

Where required, configuration information **should** *be accessible for users, customers, suppliers and partners to assist them in their planning and decision making. For example, an external service provider may make configuration information accessible to the customer and other parties to support the other service management processes for the end-to-end service.*

Configuration management reports **should** *be available to all relevant parties. The reports* **should** *cover the identification and status of the configuration items, their versions and*

ISO/IEC 20000-1 requirements

Master copies of digital configuration items **shall** be controlled in secure physical or electronic libraries and referenced to the configuration records, e.g. software, testing products, support documents.

All configuration items **shall** be uniquely identifiable and recorded in a CMDB to which update access **shall** be strictly controlled.

The CMDB **shall** be actively managed and verified to ensure its reliability and accuracy.

The status of configuration items, their versions, location, related changes and problems and associated documentation **shall** be visible to those who require it.

ISO/IEC 20000-1 requirements

Configuration audit procedures **shall** include recording deficiencies and initiating corrective actions and reporting on the outcome.

ISO/IEC 20000-2 recommendations (*italics*) and additional commentary (**bold**)

associated documentation.

Reports **should** *cover:*

a) latest configuration item versions;

b) location of the configuration item and for software the location of the master versions;

c) interdependencies;

d) version history;

e) status of configuration items that together constitute:

   1) service configuration or system;

   2) a change, baseline, build or release;

   3) version or variant.

Configuration verification and audit

Configuration verification and audit processes, both physical and functional, **should** *be scheduled and a check performed to ensure that adequate processes and resources are in place to:*

a) protect the physical configurations and the intellectual capital of the organization;

b) ensure that the service provider is in control of its configurations, master copies and licences;

c) provide confidence that configuration information is accurate, controlled and visible;

d) ensure that a change, a release, a system or an environment conforms to its contracted

ISO/IEC 20000-1 requirements

ISO/IEC 20000-2 recommendations (*italics*) and additional commentary (**bold**)

or specified requirements and that the configuration records are accurate.

*Configuration audits **should** be carried out regularly, before and after major change, after a disaster and at random intervals.*

*Deficiencies and non-conformities **should** be recorded, assessed and corrective action initiated, acted upon and fed back to the relevant parties and plan for improving the service.*

NOTE Normally there are two types of configuration audits:

a) functional configuration audit: a formal examination to verify that a configuration item has achieved the performance and functional characteristics specified in its configuration documents;

b) physical configuration audit: a formal examination of the "as-built/produced" configuration of a configuration item to verify that it conforms to its product configuration documents

Table A.2 – ISO/IEC 20000 requirements with informative commentary/guidance

ISO/IEC 20000-1 requirements	ISO/IEC 20000-2 recommendations (*italics*) and additional commentary (**bold**)
Clause 9.2 Change management	
Objective: To ensure all changes are assessed, approved, implemented and reviewed in a controlled manner	
Service and infrastructure changes **shall** have a clearly defined and documented scope.	***Planning and implementing*** *The change management processes and procedures* **should** *ensure that:* *a) changes have a clearly defined and documented scope;* *b) only changes that provide business benefit are approved, e.g. commercial, legal, regulatory, statutory;* *c) changes are scheduled based on priority and risk;* *d) changes to configurations can be verified during change implementation;* *e) the time to implement changes is monitored and improved where required;*
All requests for change **shall** be recorded and classified, e.g. urgent, emergency, major, minor.	*f) it can be demonstrated how a change is:* *1) raised, recorded and classified (with references to documents that gave rise to the change);* *2) assessed for the impact, urgency, cost, benefits and risk of the changes on the service, customer and release plans;* *3) reversed or remedied if unsuccessful;* *4) documented, e.g. the change request is linked to affected CIs and the updated version of the implementation and release plans;*

ISO/IEC 20000-2 recommendations (*italics*) and additional commentary (**bold**)

5) *approved or rejected by a change authority, depending on the type, size and risk of change;*

6) *be implemented by the nominated owner within the groups responsible for the components being changed;*

7) *tested, verified and signed off;*

8) *closed and reviewed;*

9) *scheduled, monitored and reported on;*

10) *linked to incident, problem, other change and CI records where appropriate.*

The status of changes and scheduled implementation dates **should** *be used as the basis for change and release scheduling.*

Scheduling information **should** *be made available to the people affected by the change.*

Where an outage can be caused during normal service hours the people affected **should** *agree to the change before implementation.*

ISO/IEC 20000-1 requirements

Requests for changes **shall** be assessed for their risk, impact and business benefit.

The change management process **shall** include the manner in which the change **shall** be reversed or remedied if unsuccessful.

ISO/IEC 20000-1 requirements

Changes **shall** be approved and then checked, and **shall** be implemented in a controlled manner.

All changes **shall** be reviewed for success and any actions taken after implementation.

There **shall** be policies and procedures to control the authorization and implementation of emergency changes.

ISO/IEC 20000-2 recommendations (*italics*) and additional commentary (**bold**)

Closing and reviewing the change request

*All changes **should** be reviewed for success or failure after implementation and any improvements recorded. e.g. success, partial, failure; scope, time, cost, quality measures*

*A post-implementation review **should** be undertaken for major changes to check that:*

a) the change met its objectives;

b) the customers are happy with the results; e.g. via a survey

c) there have been no unexpected side effects.

*Any nonconformity **should** be recorded and actioned.*

*Any weaknesses or deficiencies identified in a review of the change management process **should** be fed into plans for improving the service.*

Emergency changes

*Emergency changes are sometimes required and where possible the change process **should** be followed but some details may be documented retrospectively. Where the emergency process bypasses other change management requirements, the change **should** conform to these requirements as soon as practicable.*

*Emergency changes **should** be justified by the implementer and reviewed after the change to verify that it was a true emergency.*

ISO/IEC 20000-1 requirements	ISO/IEC 20000-2 recommendations (*italics*) and additional commentary (**bold**)
The scheduled implementation dates of changes **shall** be used as the basis for change and release scheduling. A schedule that contains details of all the changes approved for implementation and their proposed implementation dates **shall** be maintained and communicated to relevant parties.	
Change records **shall** be analyzed regularly to detect increasing levels of changes, frequently recurring types, emerging trends and other relevant information. The results and conclusions drawn from change analysis **shall** be recorded.	***Change management reporting, analysis and actions*** *Change records **should** be analyzed regularly to detect increasing levels of changes, frequently recurring types, emerging trends and other relevant information.* *The results and conclusions drawn from change analysis **should** be recorded and acted upon.*
Actions for improvement identified from change management **shall** be recorded and input into a plan for improving the service.	

Table A.3 – ISO/IEC 20000 requirements with informative commentary/guidance

ISO/IEC 20000-1 requirements	ISO/IEC 20000-2 recommendations (*italics*) and additional commentary (**bold**)
Clause 10.1 Release management *Objective: To deliver, distribute and track one or more changes in a release into the live environment*	
NOTE The release management process **should** be integrated with the configuration and change management processes.	
The release policy stating the frequency and type of releases **shall** be documented and agreed.	*General* *Release management **should** coordinate the activities of the service provider, many suppliers and the business to plan and deliver a release across a distributed environment.* *Good planning and management are essential to package and successfully distribute a release, and to manage the associated impact and risks to the business and IT. The release of affected information systems, infrastructure, services and documentation **should** be planned with the business.* *All associated updates to documentation **should** be included in the release, e.g. business processes, support documents and service level agreements.* *The impact of all new or changed CIs required to effect the authorized changes **should** be assessed.* *The service provider **should** ensure that both technical and non technical aspects of the release are considered together.*

ISO/IEC 20000-2 recommendations (*italics*) and additional commentary (**bold**)

*The release items **should** be traceable and secure from modification. Only suitably tested and approved releases **should** be accepted into the live environment.*

Release policy

*There **should** be a release policy that includes the:*

a) frequency and type of release;

b) roles and responsibilities for release management;

c) authority for the release into acceptance test and production environments;

d) unique identification and description of all releases;

e) approach to grouping changes into a release;

f) approach to automating the build, installation, release distribution processes to aid repeatability and efficiency;

g) verification and acceptance of a release.

Release and roll out planning

*The service provider **should** work with the business to ensure that the configuration items that are to be released are compatible with each other and with configurations items in the target environment.*

*Release planning **should** ensure that the changes to affected information systems, infrastructure, services and documentation are agreed, authorized, scheduled, coordinated and tracked.*

*The release and roll out **should** be planned in stages as details of the roll out might not be*

ISO/IEC 20000-1 requirements

The service provider **shall** plan with the business the release of services, systems, software and hardware.

Plans on how to roll out the release **shall** be agreed and authorized by all relevant parties, e.g. customers, users, operations and support staff.

The process **shall** include the manner in which the release **shall** be reversed or remedied if unsuccessful.

Plans **shall** record the release dates and deliverables and

ISO/IEC 20000-1 requirements	ISO/IEC 20000-2 recommendations (*italics*) and additional commentary (**bold**)
refer to related change requests, known errors and problems. The release management process **shall** pass suitable information to the incident management process.	*known initially. The planning for a release and roll out* **should** *typically include:* *a) release dates and description of deliverables;* *b) related changes, problems and known errors closed or resolved by this release and known errors that have been identified during testing of the release;* *c) related processes to implement a release across all business and geographical units;* *d) the manner in which the release will be backed-out or remedied if unsuccessful;* *e) verification and acceptance process;* *f) communication, preparation, documentation and training for customer and support staff;* *g) logistics and processes to purchase, store, dispatch, connect, accept and dispose of goods;* *h) support resources required to ensure service levels are maintained;* *i) the identification of dependencies, related changes and associated risks that might affect the smooth transfer of a release into the acceptance test and production environments;* *j) release sign off;* *k) schedule of audits of the production environment where required for major upgrades to ensure that the live environment is in the expected state when the release is installed.*

ISO/IEC 20000-1 requirements	ISO/IEC 20000-2 recommendations (*italics*) and additional commentary (**bold**)
Requests for change **shall** be assessed for their impact on release plans. Release management procedures **shall** include the updating and changing of configuration information and change records. Emergency releases **shall** be managed according to a defined process that interfaces to the emergency change management process.	***Developing or acquiring software*** *Information systems and software releases from in-house teams, systems builders, system integrators or other organizations* **should** *be verified on receipt.* *The overall process* **should** *be documented in the configuration management plan.* ***Design, build and configure release*** *Release and distribution* **should** *be designed and implemented to:* *a) conform with the service provider's systems architecture, service management and infrastructure standards;* *b) ensure the integrity is maintained during build, installation, handling, packaging and delivery;* *c) use software libraries and related repositories to manage and control components during the build and release process;* *d) risks are clearly identified and remedial action can be taken if required;* *e) enable verification that the target platform satisfies prerequisites before installation;* *f) enable verification that a release is complete when it reaches its destination.* *The outputs from this process* **should** *include release notes, installation instructions, installed software and hardware with related configuration baseline.* *The outputs from the release* **should** *be handed over to the group responsible for testing.* *Build, installation, release and distribution processes might be automated to reduce errors, ensure that the process is repeatable and that new releases can be rolled out quickly.*

ISO/IEC 20000-1 requirements	ISO/IEC 20000-2 recommendations (*italics*) and additional commentary (**bold**)
A controlled acceptance test environment **shall** be established to build and test all releases prior to distribution.	
Release and distribution **shall** be designed and implemented so that the integrity of hardware and software is maintained during installation, handling, packaging and delivery.	***Release verification and acceptance*** *The end result* **should** *be a sign-off on completeness of the whole release package against requirements.* *The verification and acceptance processes* **should**: *a) verify that the controlled acceptance test environment matches the requirements of target production environment;* *b) ensure that the release is created from versions under configuration management and installed in the acceptance test environment using the planned production process;* *c) verify that the appropriate level of testing has been completed, e.g. functional and nonfunctional testing, business acceptance testing, testing of the build, release, distribution and installation procedures;* *d) ensure that the release is tested to the satisfaction of business customers and service provider staff;* *e) ensure that the appropriate release authority signs off each stage of acceptance testing;* *f) verify that the target platform satisfies the hardware and software prerequisites before installation;* *g) verify that a release is complete when it reaches its destination.*

ISO/IEC 20000-1 requirements

ISO/IEC 20000-2 recommendations (*italics*) and additional commentary (**bold**)

Documentation

Appropriate documentation **should** *be available on completion and stored under configuration management against the released configuration item. This documentation* **should** *include:*

a) support documentation e.g. service level agreements;

b) support documentation, e.g. system overview, installation and support procedures, diagnostic aids, operating and administration instructions;

c) build, release, installation and distribution processes;

d) contingency and back-out plans;

e) training schedule for service management, support staff and customers;

f) a configuration baseline for the release including associated CIs such as system g) documentation, test environments, test documentation, versions of build and development tools;

g) related changes, problems and known errors;

h) evidence of release authorization and related evidence of verification and acceptance.

A system or service which does not completely conform to its specified requirements **should** *be identified and recorded through configuration management and problem management prior to going live.*

Information on known errors **should** *be communicated to incident management.*

If the release is rejected, delayed or cancelled, change management **should** *be informed.*

ISO/IEC 20000-2 recommendations (*italics*) and additional commentary (bold)

Roll out, distribution and installation

The roll out plan **should** *be reviewed and detail added as necessary to ensure that all necessary activities will be performed.*

It is important that the release is delivered safely to its destination in its expected state. The roll out, distribution and installation processes **should** *ensure that:*

a) all hardware and software storage areas are secure;

b) there are appropriate procedures for the storage, dispatch, receipt and disposal of goods;

c) installation, environmental, electrical and facilities checks are planned and completed;

d) that business and service provider staff are notified of new releases;

e) redundant products, services and licences are decommissioned.

After software distribution over a network it is essential to check that the release is complete and operational when it reaches its destination.

After a successful installation the asset and configuration management records **should** *be updated with the location and the owner of the hardware and software.*

An installation customer acceptance and satisfaction questionnaire may be used to record success or failure. Results of any customer surveys **should** *be fed back to business relationship management.*

ISO/IEC 20000-1 requirements

ISO/IEC 20000-1 requirements

Success and failure of releases **shall** be measured. Measurements **shall** include incidents related to a release in the period following a release.

Analysis **shall** include assessment of the impact on the business, IT operations and support staff resources, and **shall** provide input to a plan for improving the service.

ISO/IEC 20000-2 recommendations (*italics*) and additional commentary (**bold**)

Post release and roll out

The number of incidents related to the release in the period immediately following a roll out **should** *be measured and analyzed to assess their impact on the business, operations and support staff resources.*

The change management process **should** *include a post-implementation review.*

Recommendations **should** *be fed into a plan for improving the service.*

APPENDIX B

Bibliography and further information

Standards

BS 0-3, *A standard for standards — Part 3: Specification for structure, drafting and presentation*

ISO 9000, *Quality management systems — Fundamentals and vocabulary*

ISO 9001, *Quality management systems — Requirements*

ISO/IEC 17799, *Information technology — Security techniques — Code of practice for information security management*

ISO/IEC 20000-1, *Information technology — Service management — Part 1: Specification*

ISO/IEC 20000-2, *Information technology — Service management — Part 2: Code of practice*

ISO/IEC 27001, *Information technology — Security techniques — Information security management systems — Requirements*

BSI books

BIP 0005, *A manager's guide to service management*

BIP 0015, *IT service management — Self-assessment workbook*

BIP 0008, *Code of practice for legal admissibility and evidential weight of information stored electronically*

PAS 56, *Guide to business continuity management*

Security information

BIP 0070, *Information security compilation on CD-ROM*

BIP 0071, *Guidelines on requirements and preparation for certification based on ISO/IEC 27001*

BIP 0072, *Are you ready for an ISMS audit based on ISO/IEC 27001?*

BIP 0073, *Guide to the implementation and auditing of ISMS controls based on ISO/IEC 27001*

BIP 0074, *Measuring the effectiveness of your ISMS implementations based on ISO/IEC 27001*

Other resources

British Computer Society: www.bcs.org.uk

British Computer Society Configuration Management Specialist Group: www.bcs-cmsg.org.uk

The IT Service Management Forum (itSMF): www.itsmf.com

EXIN: www.exin.nl

Information Systems Examinations Board (ISEB): www.bcs.org.uk/iseb

The Office of Government Commerce: www.ogc.gov.uk

IT Infrastructure Library (ITIL): www.itil.co.uk

Books in the
'Achieving ISO/IEC 20000' series

There are ten books in the 'Achieving ISO/IEC 20000' series. Each book in the series includes an abstract of ISO/IEC 20000 that is most relevant to the topic of the book, as well as useful contacts and sources of supporting information. These books can be purchased through the BSI website at www.bsi-global.com.

BIP 0030, *Management decisions and documentation*

This book covers: the background to ISO/IEC 20000; a comparison to other standards and best practice material; compliance and certification audits; the scope of service management; building the business case for achieving ISO/IEC 20000; preparation for an audit and using ISO/IEC 20000 to select your supplier. Important terms that are used in management system standards, where the exact meaning of terms is important to the correct interpretation of the standard, are also explained, including the differences between the terms '**shall**', '**should**' and notes. This book also covers the requirements and recommendations for documents and records, which is a management responsibility requirement in clause 3.2 of ISO/IEC 20000-1.

BIP 0031, *Why people matter*

This book covers the roles and responsibilities of management and process owners, and explains the importance of management commitment to best practice service management, mapping onto the requirements and recommendations of clause 3.1 of ISO/IEC 20000, *Management responsibility*. The book also covers the importance of motivation, training and career development as well as tips and techniques, mapping onto the requirements of clause 3.3 of ISO/IEC 20000-1, *Competence, awareness and training*.

BIP 0032, *Making metrics work*

This book gives a practical view of why metrics and service reports are so important to the delivery of an effective service and to service improvements. It describes the types, the design, target audiences and documentation of metrics used in the service reporting process, covered by the requirements of clauses 4 and 6.2 of ISO/IEC 20000-1, *Plan-Do-Check-Act (PDCA) cycle* and *Service reporting*. Useful tips, techniques and example metrics are included.

BIP 0033, *Managing end-to-end service*

This book describes the supply chains that are commonly managed by service level management, business relationship management and supplier management, which are the requirements in clauses 6.1 and 7 of ISO/IEC 20000-1. It describes the interfaces between suppliers, the service provider and one or many customers. This book also includes useful tips for aspects of end-to-end service, such as the role of service level agreements (SLAs), service reviews, customer satisfaction and complaints procedures.

BIP 0034, *Finance for service managers*

This book covers *Budgeting and accounting for IT services* based on clause 6.4 of ISO/IEC 20000. It introduces financial terms that may be unfamiliar to service management specialists, which will help with understanding the requirements and recommendations. It also covers the relationship between budgeting, accounting and charging, and outlines the importance of service management processes in regulatory compliance.

BIP 0035, *Enabling change*

This book covers the configuration, change management and release management processes which are contained in clauses 9 and 10 of ISO/IEC 20000. It compares the three processes and describes how they interface with each other, and gives advice on the requirements and recommendations of ISO/IEC 20000, example metrics and audit evidence. This book also includes practical advice on meeting the ISO/IEC 20000 requirements on the roles and responsibilities of those involved.

BIP 0036, *Keeping the service going*

This book covers the service continuity and availability management, incident management and problem management processes, which are contained in clauses 6.3 and 8 of ISO/IEC 20000. It explains the role of these processes in keeping the customer's service going, ranging from continuity planning through to the fast-fixing of incidents. It compares the processes and describes how they interface with each other. It includes example metrics and audit evidence, with practical tips and techniques that will help a service provider achieve the requirements.

BIP 0037, *Capacity management*

This book covers the requirements for the capacity management process in clause 6.5 of ISO/IEC 20000. It describes the capacity management process and its role as a link between business plans, workloads, capacity and performance). It also covers the planning required to ensure a service provider is able to deliver a service that allows the customer's business to operate effectively. The book describes capacity management for all types of resources within the scope of service management.

BIP 0038, *Integrated service management*

The opening paragraph of ISO/IEC 20000-1 states that '*This standard promotes the adoption of an integrated process approach to effectively deliver managed services to meet the business and customer requirements*'. This book reflects the importance placed by ISO/IEC 20000 on understanding the interfaces between processes, and how the interfaces are managed so that service management processes are fully integrated. It also reflects the top-down management system approach that is fundamental to ISO/IEC 20000. This book describes how understanding and meeting the requirements of ISO/IEC 20000 gives better control, greater efficiency and opportunities for improvements.

BIP 0039, *The differences between BS 15000 and ISO/IEC 20000*

This book will be of particular interest to those who have used BS 15000 for service improvements, audits or training and need to update their material to reflect the ISO/IEC 20000 standard. ISO/IEC 20000 was based on BS 15000, and this book provides a detailed comparison of ISO/IEC 20000 and BS 15000, for both Parts 1 and 2. It shows the differences in structure, clause numbering and references. The core of this book is a series of tables detailing the changes to the requirements and recommendations clause-by-clause, as well as any re-wording that has been provided to give clarification for an international audience. It includes an explanation of why the changes were made and the implications of each of the changes. This book is based on the material produced by the Project Editor during the drafting of both Parts 1 and 2 of ISO/IEC 20000.